Your New Beginning

Saving The World

GABRIELA QUEEN

Dedication

I want to thank *Lucas*. You are the light of my life and my inspiration. Thanks for your help and for giving me the strength to finish the book. Without you, this book will not be possible.

Introduction

This is a self-help and self-improvement book that contains wisdom and the true meaning of life. The life that we should live when we know that it is possible.

Lucas and his friends are looking for a New Beginning in their lives. On this amazing journey, Lucas finds a way to help his friends and the World.

This is a story of Hope based on a reality that can be achieved with logic and wisdom from the invisible but Real World.

The invisible will be known. Be ready for Your New Beginning.

Prologue

Open your eye to the things of The Unknown, which will transform you.

There is always a way to know about the treasures of this World.

When you know the 'secrets' and you follow them, then you will arrive at the end of Your New Beginning.

Start your search TODAY.

Chapter 1
Your Divine POWER

T his world is not the world we are meant to live in. It is full of envy, evil, anger, depression, unfaithfulness, criticism, quarrels, pains, sicknesses, and shame.

Nevertheless, there is another World, that I will call 'Paradise'. This is not a specific place but you need to find it within yourself.

Many people wrongly believe that you will be in Paradise after death, but that place is on earth, here and now.

Many have tried to deny it. However, what is in your mind can become a reality. If you desire and search wisdom it will be manifested in you.

You can see a glimpse of Paradise and it is within you. The way to find it and manifest it is in this way:

- First of all, and most important is that you need to search for Wisdom. Wisdom comes only from The Divine.

If you understand that the impossible is possible and that what is real is the 'other world', then it will manifest.

Everything you have ever wanted will become reality and the negative thoughts will go away when you will know reality.

Your beliefs have to be transformed and shaped so that your new ideas will manifest into a marvellous reality.

It is something that you should practice day by day, night by night, minute by minute. You need to *extract* the wrong and negative beliefs and teachings.

There has to be no doubt in your mind, so you will not lose your way.

You need wisdom and logic to manifest this Paradise in conjunction with The Divine's help.

Some thoughts and beliefs have to be completely different to achieve this. You need to 'reset' your mind.

Many things you were taught have to be transformed, and moulded and many that you never thought were true, have to change for a *new reality*.

Nobody can tell you what to think, or what to do in your life. Search for things that are logical and rational. You need to ask yourself many questions so that you can arrive at a different outcome.

Don't just accept what people say as a fact but ask questions. No matter who that person is.

You need to take a *different path*. Don't follow the same thoughts and beliefs that took you nowhere. You need to break the circle.

Then, these new logical ideas will be forming your new thoughts so that you will know who you really are and you can be in 'Paradise'.

When you can detach yourself from every negativity, negative people, wrong beliefs, anger, and past pains only then you will be able to create new and good thoughts.

These thoughts will bring you to a New Beginning.

When you know that you can fight against all desires and vices, you will arrive at that Paradise.

Words

Spoken and written words are very powerful. If you want to hurt someone you will say negative words and if you want to make someone feel good you will say positive words.

It is also important to know the proper meaning of words to express the correct idea.

The word hell is similar to the sound of the word 'head'. That's why hell is in your head, in your mind, and in your thoughts.

Hell is not a place underground; it is the negative *thoughts* that you may have that will bring negative outcomes and negative people.

'Heaven' is in your head too. They are both in the same place. You need to get rid of the negative thoughts which is hell.

So that, you arrive in 'Heaven' or 'Paradise'; and have positive thoughts.

When you find peace in your mind then you have peace to search for Wisdom. But if you have negative thoughts, that will be your hell and you can't focus on wisdom or anything.

Evil people are lovers of evil, consciously and willingly and it is in their minds all the time. They follow wrong ideas and wrong beliefs, they lack love.

On the other hand, good people do good things, rejoice with justice, and love, which is The Divine's essence.

People with love will be in Paradise.

You need to find peace in your head and have positive thoughts. This will be achieved with knowledge, logic, understanding, and wisdom.

You need to search for these things. These things are hidden from us.

You need a clear and peaceful mind to have time to contemplate your thoughts.

When negative thoughts, people, or situations arise in your life, you need wisdom to overcome them. We need to know what to do and what to say so that we win every evil against us.

It is worth it to learn how to overcome these 'powers' or negative thoughts. These 'powers' are also persons with a form called a body, a vessel and they are like wolves in sheep's clothing.

But do not worry.

The way to win these entities is to learn how to get wisdom from The Divine. Make the connection and life will flourish.

Therefore, to go to Paradise you need to extract all the negative thoughts and find new ones through wisdom.

An analogy of this will be; if you have a suitcase full of old and dirty clothes. Old and dirty clothes are your negative mindset.

Therefore, you need to let go of negative thoughts. You need new and clean clothes; a new mindset.

You need to block the 'negative thoughts' in your mind.

These negative thoughts later will make you feel sad, angry, depressed, or sick.

These are the negativity or bad frequencies that disturb your peace. Then you start having negative thoughts even without realising you have them.

These thoughts then can become your reality.

Words are vibrations, frequencies, or modulations. They have the power to do good things or to destroy.

Your 'Words' will be manifested into existence in this world. Because your words will *send a signal* to your mind.

From there something will happen, you will put it into action and then it will be manifested.

Therefore, be careful what you wish and what you say.

If you remove the *letter L* in the word 'w-o-r-l-d-'. Then you will have the word 'w-o-r-d'.

The creation of YOUR world is with YOUR words. Words are beliefs as well.

Your body is vibrating, and your brain and your heart are vibrating constantly like everything in the Universe.

Therefore, the vibration should be positive so that will be a positive reality.

Before you speak you have a thought and then what you were thinking will come into words. Your thoughts, beliefs, and words make your reality.

We need positive thoughts that will bring positive *words* with positive vibrations. This will bring a New Reality.

∞ ∞ ∞

Wisdom

Wisdom gives you the right reality. You will have positive vibrations that will help to overcome bad vibrations.

Wisdom is necessary to find yourself. And when you will find wisdom you will find The Divine within you, and you will find yourself.

You will find power when you will know that you are free. You don't need to become free. You need to KNOW you are free. Know yourself through wisdom and logic.

DESCARTES SAID, 'I THINK, THEREFORE I AM'.

But I understand this as:

'I'M THINKING, THEREFORE I EXIST.'

I can also understand this as:

'I know, then I am.'

When you **know** who you really are, then you can manifest it.

You have Power. This is **A FACT**.

Chapter 2

Where is your Soul?
Where is the Signal?

If we do an analogy, and we say that our body is a radio, the antenna is our third eye to communicate.
The signal of the radio is our soul.

Then, we can say that the signal comes from The Divine, the main source of power.
On the other hand, on the radio, the signal comes from the broadcast.

'The pineal gland is associated with the sixth chakra, called also the 'third eye' located between your eyebrows, essentially deep back in your brain.'

Many people will not know about the pineal gland, that we have in our head.

In the analogy, the radio doesn't have a signal inside of the radio itself.

However, if we take apart all the components of the radio you can't see the signal but that doesn't mean there is no signal.

13

When you switch it off, you can't hear anything. That doesn't mean the signal doesn't exist.

Because when you switch it on you can hear the signal again.

Therefore, we can conclude that there is a signal coming from the broadcast to the radio when we switch it on.

In consequence, we can say that we have a soul (signal) to communicate with The Divine (the broadcast). That makes us alive (switch on).

However, it has to be tuned, if not it will be unmodulated and it will not have a good reception so it will be noisy, and chaotic.

If it is switched off there is no signal but if you switch it on the signal will be there.

Switch on your signal (**your soul**) and you will get wisdom from the Divine.

Your signal will be turned on and you will have an excellent reception and peace.

Start afresh with your New life, your New Beginning.

Start afresh

To start afresh and have a transformation we need to learn new things and leave old beliefs.

We should get rid of some of our old thoughts, ideas, teachings, and beliefs - this will be a process.

It takes time to change your thoughts, and also the ideas and beliefs that you have learned all your life.

These are indoctrinations from schools, universities, friends, television, movies, family and religions.

Many were indoctrinated as well, it is not their fault because they didn't know better. But now we need to search for the right signal to get wisdom.

Seeds

You are like a seed. The seed that was sown in good soil has to explode to have life. The seed case has to split to allow the roots and stem to emerge and grow.

Until then it is just a seed with only the potential to be a plant and it will not produce and harvest until it is watered.

You are the seed. You need to learn how to explode to emerge and grow so that you give fruits for the harvest.

When you know the life that you should live and you desire it then it will be manifested. You need to have wisdom for you to be fruitful.

You can learn how to have wisdom through a connection with the 'Source' The Divine.

I hope you know that the impossible is possible. Also, you need to give less attention to earthly and materialistic things and learn about the unknown that can be known.

You should know that you *are free* from any authority because nobody owns you. Nobody can or should think for you. Nobody can or should decide for you.

Nobody should put beliefs on you.

Most people don't want to talk or read about the unknown because is different from their beliefs. These different beliefs will then be classified as unreal.

The idea will be rejected as untrue so that people will disbelieve. Also, the idea will be called 'false belief', which is a negative connotation to reinforce someone's idea to be left as false.

Words were used to confuse people and think differently. If they do, they will be rejected with negative words and shame.

However, you need to ask yourself questions about everything they taught you. Ask questions to the Divine and wait for His wisdom.

Ask yourself why they teach the same subjects in every country of the world and they don't allow questioning these 'beliefs'.

These things are taught from a very early age so that you won't forget them and take them through all your life as your own beliefs.

You think they are YOUR beliefs, and you won't ask questions and you won't try to change them.

Also, it will be difficult for you to believe something different because you have these beliefs for many years embedded in your mind.

You should think that maybe there is more to life than eating, drinking, having material things, having children, etc. You should:

'SEARCH AND YOU WILL FIND' MATTHEW 7:7

What do you need to search and find?

Having different perspectives makes you think. They don't want you to think and ask questions. Try to ask questions and you will see what will happen.

Then, you will discover things that are not as they told you.

Treasures of life

Treasures are difficult to find because they are hidden. You need many clues to arrive at the treasure. You need to learn to find the clues like in a treasure hunt.

The treasure is within YOU. Find yourself, find who you are.

If you don't try new ideas, you will never know new things. Always try what resonates with you and if you fail try again until you get it right.

Some people are so busy with life that they don't have time to stop and think about what Life is.

They don't try to communicate with The Divine or they don't think they are worthy or they think that they can't do it.

Many people focus on money, work, friends, holidays, and family which are their priorities. When all these things will be gone, what will be left of all this?

Many people work so hard for the future, but who knows about the future?

You should think about the only thing that brings a solution to all your problems.

These things are: Eternal Peace, Perfect Love, and Happiness.

Nobody can buy these things in the supermarket. You need time to search and find them.

Only The Divine can provide you with wisdom to give you these treasures. These things are spiritual things not physical.

They are abstract things are not achieved by physical things.

You should yearn for these things that are the*essence* of life.

In this example, in Luke 10:38-42 you will see how busy people can be and as a result, they lost what is important in life. Martha lost it.

Jesus went to visit Martha and Maria in their house. Martha was busy cooking a great meal for him but Maria was sitting down listening to Jesus wisdom.

Martha was angry because she was busy and she said to Jesus that Maria should help her.

Jesus answered, 'Maria has chosen the most important thing in life.'

Maria wanted to learn about The Unknown, she needed to know about The Divine. She was not interested in food at that time because it was not important for her eternal life.

Martha didn't understand this, she was thinking about food, instead of thinking about Spiritual or Unknown things.

You need to be like Maria, you need to yearn for wisdom for the unknown and find your Power.

Contemplate nature and connect with it as we are part of everything, everything is ONE. Know Thyself.

You are not a body, you are not just what you see in the mirror and that is why you need to know who you really are.

You shouldn't identify yourself with the description of your body, house, title, country, or surname.

You need to connect with the Source of wisdom to identify yourself and realise who you are.

Knowing the unknown is knowing thyself.

You are not what they told you that you are. You have a spirit/soul that makes you alive. You need to feed the spirit with spiritual food and water like Maria.

John 21:6 says,

'CAST YOUR NET ON THE RIGHT-HAND SIDE AND YOU WILL FIND FISH. SO IF YOU DO IT, YOU WILL NOT BE ABLE TO HAUL IT IN BECAUSE OF THE NUMBER OF FISH'

I understand this like this:

YOU will find YOURSELF (fish) when you will feed your spirit with spiritual things.

Then, you will find many BLESSINGS (many fish) when you will know yourself.

I think, that in this passage when he talks about the right side is the right side of your mind. Also, I think it means that you need to go to the right path.

Therefore, this means that you are on the wrong path, which is the one that you have been taught. Certain beliefs that are half-truths.

It is saying that you need to change your beliefs and don't go left, go right.

You need to know and understand things rather than have beliefs based on half-truths and no logic.

I think, the word 'fish' can also mean **Wisdom** and you need to find it on the right path. Wisdom is hidden in stories, parables and allegories.

Manifest wisdom

This is how you manifest things with wisdom. When you have positive thoughts and the right knowledge you will bring wisdom.

What are you willing to do for endless love, peace, and happiness?

Are you ready to go on a different path?

Do you want to find these treasures in your life?

You have the choice and the answer is within you. Put yourself in the first place.

Then, your heart and mind should be in perfect harmony, with love for everyone and everything around you.

In consequence, you will have ten times more of what you are waiting for. The day of your New Beginning is today.

Wisdom is logical and demonstrable.

'THE ONE CAN BE KNOWN RATHER THAN SEEN.' (PLATO)

I think, that you can know The Divine when you are ready and you decide to know rather than to follow 'beliefs'.

There is always a *choice* to make in life.

Don't lose the most important choice of your life, which is the one Maria has chosen. She chose wisdom and knowledge to know herself and to know the unknown.

Ignorance

The word ignorance in the dictionary means lack of knowledge or information.

I think it should say that is lack of *the rightknowledge* and the *right information*.

22

When you have been taught many things that are not important to the soul which doesn't help your daily life that is ignorance. It is lack of the right knowledge and the right information for a good life.

You can't solve problems in life with false information, false knowledge, or half-truths, rather you need wisdom from The Divine.

∞∞∞

The eye is the antenna

MATTHEW 6:22 SSAYS: 'THE LIGHT OF THE BODY IS THE EYE: IF THEREFORE THINE EYE BE SINGLE; THY WHOLE BODY SHALL BE FULL OF LIGHT.'

I think, that in this passage the <u>single</u> eye **is not** one of your eyes, or it would have said: *your right or left eye or one of your eyes.*

Only one eye is the light of the body.

It talks about that the eye is our *third eye*, which is called the *pineal gland.*

Therefore, this is the third eye that gives you:

Light, *Wisdom* and *Power.*

This eye makes you see things that are unknown, supernatural and spiritual. It is the antenna to communicate with the Divine.

Therefore, you can't see them with your normal eyes.

Schools and Universities don't teach or give importance to this gland.

This is hidden when you study anatomy at school.

Even doctors may know this but will not give it much importance. It will be another accessory of the body.

My question is this, why is this gland in your brain? Your mind is where you have your beliefs.

Everything in your body has a perfect functionality.

Why they don't teach about this in the anatomy class?

Why is not important to know? But you can't deny it is there.

Therefore, we should know about the functionality and as it is near the brain it should be very important to know it.

When you KNOW that you can do almost anything and you can control what comes to your mind - ***you can control your world and your reality.***

When you can control your world, you can control what you want in your life and you will make your future perfect.

You will know your *power* and you can't be controlled by beliefs. Because you will have wisdom.

Then, your diamond mind will shine and be full of Light.

Wisdom will be within you in everything you will do.

You have the connection to receive wisdom with your **eye**, that is the power to shine and be Light.

Stars shine in the darkness. You are a star and a diamond.

Let's shine as bright as never before in harmony.

And as you shine you will be in Paradise forever.

Chapter 3
Choose Light over darkness

There are two lights. One is called Light (The Divine) the other one is called illumination (electricity, the fake light).

Light is within you and nobody has seen it yet. You need not only knowledge but Wisdom to find Light.

The Divine is the Light.

Today it's the most important moment, not the past or the future.

You shouldn't remember the past because it will bring sorrow, or memories of what it was before and what it is not any more.

All these things; can make you sad because they don't exist anymore.

Generally, people think negatively, about things of the past and they must be avoided at all costs.

You also shouldn't think much about tomorrow because we don't know what will happen in the future.

Thus, if we are thinking about tomorrow we create anxiety and worry, so the best you can do is to avoid thinking about it.

Therefore, it is good to make your life as pleasant as possible. You need to do what you want every second of your day, as much as you can.

Have fun, enjoy, sing, dance, and the most important is don't let anyone destroy your life. Be grateful to The Divine.

If you cry about something that didn't happen yet; you will cry twice.

Don't cry in the present, and the second time in the future when that particular thing will happen. If it will happen.

Therefore, this will be double suffering, double stress and double anger. The future may not be as bad as you may think that would be or it may not happen at all.

Don't cry twice and don't worry but think about the future positively always.

Look at another example:
If you have to go to the dentist and you are afraid before going to the dentist because you think you will be in pain, then you will have double stress.

You will stress before going to the dentist and when you are there.

Just think about the present and not about the future or you will have double suffering. Because nobody knows about the future and maybe it will be different so then you worried about nothing.

To learn how to live a 'Paradise' life, you must learn a very important life lesson which is to have a lot of patience.

You need a balance in life and you need to know what to do, when to do it and how to do it.

This comes only from wisdom and the only way to have wisdom is by knowing yourself, knowing the power within, your Divine power.

You already have in you the ability to know good and bad and you don't need anyone to teach you this.

With the Divine's help, you will know what to do every time. He is The Power, the power within you.

Therefore, you need to have wisdom and at the right time, you will have it. You should try many times to achieve what you want or you will never know the outcome if you stop trying and searching.

After learning and grasping how to be patient, you will understand the beauty of patience. Nobody knows about the future, so if you live with wisdom, you can have a happy future.

For that reason, you need the patience to build the present. Also, you need to shape your present to have a better future.

You can shape things that are not perfect with wisdom.

You can't expect to receive what you don't know.

You can't know what you don't search and ask. You need to do a research and study like an essay to find wisdom.

When you finished your research you will have a better knowledge.

In the dictionary the word 'to know' means **absolute knowledge.**

You can only have **absolute knowledge** when you asked yourself all the questions and you received the wisdom to answer them.

If *someone else* gave you the answers it is not *your* knowledge and it may not be teh absolute knowledge.

In the word 'knowledge' you have the word 'know'.

You will KNOW the truth....

Think about the Light

You are not your body, mind, and thoughts. You are more than that. That is just a visual description of yourself. That is not how a blind person will describe you.

Love yourself first, love everything about yourself, and don't punish yourself for anything that you did wrong.

There are no mistakes, everything is a step to the next level in your life.

We are learning every second, and making mistakes is part of the learning. With wisdom, you will have a way to solve problems that others can't.

You have to be in perfect harmony, love, and patience. You can shape anything with the power of love. Because The Divine is Love, the real and perfect love.

It is your choice.

You have the power within you. When you know your power, then it will bring many changes in you and your surroundings.

You are Divine, Light and Power not just a body.

You are 'no-body'. This means you are not a body.

After you **know** your power you will see that things, situations and people will make your life better. Some people will give you what you need or tell you an easy way to do what you need.

Wisdom will come to you.

Hence, *knowing* your power will attract the solution for you. Your wisdom and knowledge have power, use it positively.

Search how to know who you really are.

The Divine within will be manifested in you. Have patience you will see it and it will develop day by day.

Do not stop searching for wisdom and knowledge, because what you say and what you think will come to pass.

You don't need to be troubled, afraid, or worried about anything because these emotions are bad for your heart and mind.

Don't listen to negative things or negative people.

Focus and search for your power and you will find it.

Therefore, you will find peace and love. Because that is who you are.

Your Light will shine in darkness and the darkness of this life will disappear.

Darkness means **lack of** light or **absence of** light.

When you will be full of Light, there will be no more darkness.

Open the door for wisdom and switch on YOUR LIGHT to see your New Beginning.

Chapter 4

Be 'LIGHT'

Y ou should write YOUR own story with a beautiful beginning and with NO END.

Write it in your mind with new thoughts. You can write it and draw it as a reminder. Act upon it in consequence, and never stop until it happens.

SHAKESPEARE SAID, 'TO BE OR NOT TO BE?'

What does it mean for you?

What do you have to **be**?

What do you have to **not be**?

I think, that this means that you need to **be** someone that you are not. Therefore, do **not be** what you believe, or what someone made you believe that you are.

In other words, you need to **be Light** and **(not be)** just a **body**.

The verb to be 'SER'

In Spanish, the verb to be is translated into two ways, 'Ser' and 'Estar'. Estar is used with temporary statements.

But SER is used with *permanent statements* such as I am a woman or I am a man. It is used with things that are permanent and **do not change**.

Translation in Spanish:
'To be or not to be?' you will use the verb *Ser* like this:

'SER O NO SER?'

You will use the verb SER in this sentence because it means that we are not temporary beings but we are *permanent beings*, we won't die.

The same will occur in Italian if we translate it:
'Essere o non Essere'.

There are two different verbs in Italian that can be used with the verb 'to be' for other meanings, you use 'Stare'.

However, some people will believe that they can die. It is partly true; it is called half-true. There are many half-truths in this world.

You don't die, only your vessel dies, which is your _body_ but not who we are.

Some people can also be dead because their minds are dead.

I know for a fact that my mind was dead when I didn't know who I am.

Therefore, I was spiritually dead. I was controlled by the programming beliefs that I learned from childhood. They programmed me in my house, school, university, etc.

But as soon as I had wisdom and knew the power I have and where this power is coming from, I knew who I am.

Only then I was alive. I could see a New Beginning for me. The Light within me and The Divine's wisdom came to me.

I also knew how to make my days wonderful at every second.

Every day is amazing and so full of new things, with extremely gratifying things. Because every day is the future, every day is a New Beginning.

You can manifest your future. Sometimes it is even better than what you expected and it will become real.

Know who you are and who you are not.

What is <u>real</u> and what is <u>unreal?</u>

Which rules, beliefs and ideas are you following?

Who told you about them?

This beliefs are they always logic, fair and perfect?

Or are they unfair, imperfect and not logic?

To **know** is to **be**. And to **be** is to **know**.

<u>Knowledge symbolises a 'Cake recipe'</u>

Your *knowledge* symbolised a *cake recipe*; you need to put the right ingredients in it to make the best cake.

If you don't put the exact amount of ingredients the cake will not taste like mine. It will still be a cake but just similar with a different taste and consistency.

My cake is delicious and is the best cake ever. It took me years to find the right ingredients and to make a great recipe. I made many cakes but none like this.

If I eat it, it brings me joy and happiness.

If I eat it, it makes me smile and rejoice. I feel invincible and unstoppable… and it is also a healthy cake.

It is the healthiest of them all, and the best taste ever. It is the best of the best. As I always said, only the best for me!

You will ask me how can a cake make you feel that.

The answer is that when you **know** and have wisdom and don't doub then, it will have that effect on you.

The ingredients are The Divine, youself and His wisdom.

Knowledge is important but Wisdom is greater.

There is nothing and there is nobody that can make you happier than yourself.

YOU can make yourself happy.

The Divine is within you. Your soul is perfect and pure to make you happy. You are perfect and pure like gold.

Gold is gold, it doesn't have to be purified. It is a wrong belief. Gold is pure even if mixed with another metal, gold is gold. You need to extract the other metal.

You need to extract some beliefs.

$$\infty \infty \infty$$

Here is how you make this cake, you just need these ingredients:

LOVE

It is the first ingredient; please use it in all that you do. Love is freedom.

The other day I cooked vegetable lasagne and I decided to say aloud, 'I add *love* to the lasagne.'

After I served it, the result was what I expected. When they tried my food they loved it.

They didn't know that I put the *love* ingredient in my food. They were all saying that it was delicious and that they loved it.

They couldn't even stop eating it and they also said that it was the best I have ever cooked.

When you cook add the *love* ingredient just think about it. It doesn't cost you anything, and it takes you no time.

If you put the ingredient or not, you still have to cook. If you want it to be like mine, then you need that ingredient.

Search for the perfect love, The Divine.

∞ ∞ ∞

PATIENCE

It is the second ingredient. When you cook a meal there are two ways.

One is the fast way; in which you don't put too many ingredients. For example, you do some eggs on toast.

The other way is where you put effort and time.

First, you will need one ingredient to cook. After that, you will need another ingredient and wait for it to be cooked. Then, your last ingredient.

You also need to put the right quantity of each ingredient for the right quantity of people.

You have two*choices* here:
1)   you can cook a wonderful meal and spend time and effort.

2)   or you can just eat beans on toast.

When you have two or more options then it means that you have a choice. One option is not a choice.

Until now maybe you didn't choose your own option, then it means it was someone else option.

I would advise you to eat a tasty meal rather than having whatever is inside the fridge.

I suggest to search for wisdom and with patience at the right time, the best things will come to you.

The cake needs time to rise, and the lasagne time to cook, and this means that people also need time to learn and find the right options.

YOUR options, YOUR questions and YOUR answers.

∞ ∞ ∞

The BEST or nothing

If you are looking with your physical eyes you can't see spiritual things.

For example:
If you look into the neighbour's grass you may think it is greener than yours but maybe, that is not true. Maybe it is a half-truths.

However, it can be true if your neighbour puts a lot of effort, love and patience into that grass so that it will be the most beautiful grass in the neighbourhood.

Did you do the same with your grass (life)? We shouldn't look into our neighbour's garden; we should concentrate and focus on*our*garden.

Because we may see a fake grass with our eyes and we don't know it is fake, it seems real.

Your life is the garden and your soul is the garden.

What you say to yourself, and what you believe about yourself is your garden and it has to be treated with love.

Make your life better with a different green colour that you have never seen before. You should know yourself, love yourself and desire the BEST for your life or nothing.

Learn that you have a perfect soul. You are not your physical faults. Noting is a mistake.

You don't have to become Light rather, you *are* **Light**.

∞ ∞ ∞

The CHERRY on top

It is the last ingredient.

Finally, when you finished cooking a cake you put the cherry on top.

You need wisdom and the only way to know yourself is through wisdom, and not with your own knowledge and understanding. Neither with someone else knowledge.

You can know through wisdom and that is the main ingredient… ***to know*** without doubt.

Saint-Exupery said,

'WHAT IS ESSENTIAL IS INVISIBLE TO THE EYE.'

I think, that the 'eye' means the 'third eye'. With this eye, we can see the **invisible**, The Divine.

Also, with this eye, we will see the unknown which is the **essential** thing and it is **invisible** to the physical eyes.

You can only see invisible things which are spiritual things with the third eye. For this to happen, you need to know the unknown is real.

How can you know the unknown?

MATT. 18:3 'UNLESS YOU BE CONVERTED, AND BECOME LIKE LITTLE CHILDREN, YOU SHALL NOT ENTER INTO THE KINGDOM OF GOD'

This passage for me means that we need to be like children to understand the unknown. It is not to be childish but childlike.

Children understand the unknown because they are not manipulated by many different beliefs.

They like logic, wisdom and understanding. When you say something to children they don't doubt it because they don't have beliefs.

They understand and don't doubt in their unpolluted minds. They can understand better what they can't see with their physical eyes.

Children can understand and know the unknown.

On the other hand, adults are programmed to believe only in what they can see. They are told not to behave like children but to be adults.

However, you should be like children and you won't have any negative thoughts. You will have more fun and know things. And then, you won't worry about tomorrow.

Children can see a beautiful world that adults can't see any more.

You can become like little children to enter into the kingdom of The Divine and see beyond with your third eye.

Only then, you can live a life that is the life you should live on this earth.

The life that you should live is explained in,

JOHN 10:10 'THEY MAY HAVE LIFE AND THAT THEY MAY HAVE IT MORE ABUNDANTLY.'

This is the life you can live now with joy, love, wisdom, and peace in abundance. These are the spiritual things that no one can buy but everyone wants, needs and treasures.

The cherry on top means *to be like children*.

You can have wisdom to know who you are and the impossible will be possible.

If you worry about something in your life, it will not go or change because you worry. However, it will change when you will change.

It will change when your mind, ideas, teachings, and beliefs will change and you will have different ones. It will change when the words that you speak will be positive.

It will change when you acknowledge The Divine's power within you to make it happen.
If the sun may darken today. And you will know that you are Light, then you will shine. You will be the power to create life.

I would like you to hear Lucas' story.

Lucas also knows that everything is possible.

He will tell you his story that talks about the impossible is possible so that YOU can also know it and have an **abundant life**.

Chapter 5

Lucas Superpowers

My name is Lucas; this is the story of my destiny.

I used to read comic books with superheroes and they were dressed in colourful tight leggings costumes.

Some of them were using capes, hats and masks to cover their faces.

At the age of nine years old, I didn't know much about superheroes in my family. I didn't have a special man or a superhero.

I grew up without my father and my family never cared for me and I guess they were too busy for me.

The only superhero I know is my mother. She was a lone parent for years, in a strange country and with many difficult situations surrounding her, one after another.

I always knew she was all I had, the only figure of a superhero, a superwoman, a wonder woman. She is resilient and very intelligent, a good cook, and a sweet mum.

But what I like most is that she believes in the impossible.

During all these years she was always very happy and I saw all the victories she achieved in her life, in mine, and other people's lives.

I knew I have come to help her, but what shall I do? I thought she will always be strong and my Queen and hero.

I remember that she told me how I came to her tummy and how she knew I was there.

One day, my mother wanted me to come into this world. But for two years this didn't happen.

Many have also prayed and asked for me to come but there was no answer. However, she never gave up, and that afternoon was different from the other days.

Before the miracle happen on earth and manifested she saw me coming.

She felt a warm sensation running from her head to her toes, and she was shaking.

But the intense heat was of calmness and stillness. Suddenly, while she was awake, she saw in a vision three men and one was holding a baby.

The room lit up; these men were not common; they were messengers of good news.

They looked like angels. She knew that I will be born, a new life, a new beginning, a new hero.

After that, in the evening, she went to sleep and did not remember the vision she had before because she was very tired.

Then, she switched off the lights and closed her eyes. At that second, a light came down from heaven directly to her tummy.

She knew that the light was a falling star. At that moment she also felt that something had entered her tummy.

She told me I came to her tummy directly from the sky and then she knew she was pregnant.

There was no pain and no scar. She felt a mixture of excitement and joy.

She said that I came like lightning.

She also was sure that she was pregnant that she will have a boy and that I will be her hero. She knew that I will bring not only joy to her but her life will change as much as mine.

Besides, the way people behave and believe will also change, and many people's perspectives will change because of me. I will be a hero, a different type of hero, different from the common ones you know.

I will not be dressed in tight little trousers with bright colours. I will not fight with guns; I will never use guns; I don't like them.

I think that wars are not good because many die and nobody wins if they are dead or injured.

My mum chose my name, and after an intensive search trying to figure out what is the best option, she found the perfect name.

She decided that I my name will be <u>Lucas</u> which means <u>Luz</u> in Spanish, it means <u>Light</u> in English.

There was no better name than that. Because that is what she saw and it describes the encounter between me and my mummy.

I am the light she saw inside of her tummy. Therefore, my name couldn't have been a different one.

She told me about this story when I was very young. I can also imagine how it happened. I came as a peal of thunder and lightning, and then I arrive inside of her tummy.

It was already planned for me to be here on this earth. I came at the right time. But until this day, I didn't know exactly why I came to live on this earth.

I know that it was meant to be, that the intense vision was for a purpose, and I will do what I came for on earth.

I am a 'normal' child with a pretty 'normal' life. I have my mum and a lot of friends.

I always thought that if you want to be a superhero you need a sort of superpower, from the spiritual world. Maybe The Divine can help me to have a superpower.

I was thinking about how can I communicate with that world. There is a problem, how can I ask for some superpowers? I was wondering how can they answer my questions.

I was also thinking about what will happen if I can't have any superpowers. What kind of superhero I will be without any superpowers?

Another question in my mind is in which way can I communicate with The Divine because I only have my tablet.

Then I thought that maybe he has a phone over there to call me and that will be the best option, I can receive calls.

But I don't think I can see Him face-to-face because maybe it is not possible. I don't know if the spiritual world will come to earth just for me.

I wouldn't know what to say to Him if He comes. Maybe I will ask Him if I can have the same superpowers that He has.

I was worried because maybe he doesn't know how to use phones. My mum has a new phone and she is not very tech to know how it works. I don't know what to do.

Maybe this is not going to work.

I need help but I don't know how to communicate with Him. I don't know if my message is going to arrive in the spiritual world.

I doubt He can help me. I don't have His number or email.

Maybe He will not listen to me because I am a child. But if He answers me whom shall I say I am?

Suddenly, I heard in my mind as someone was talking to me.

'Are you Light?'

Yes, I am Light. Who is this?

The voice said, 'I will send you a helper.'

'Thanks. I know now that my dream will become real and that someone is helping me. I knew who He was, my mum called Him, 'the Divine.'

Chapter 6
I can fly

All my friends know me as Lucas. They will know I don't have superpowers.

What can I do to make them know that I am not just a child?

Suddenly, I heard the singing of a bird.

'You are not just a child' the bird said.

'Who am I if I am not a child?'

My friends can see who I am. Shall I hide my face so that they don't recognise me? If they see me they won't believe that I have superpowers.

They know I am a child and I am not a superhero with superpowers. Maybe I will change my name and put on a mask. But I don't like masks.

I want to be myself. I don't want to hide. I like who I am.

I was hearing the voice closer and closer.

'You are not just a child; you are Light.' the voice said again.

I'm confused. Am I Light? Who am I? I realised that I don't know myself very well. Of course, I am light.

At that moment, the most beautiful black and white Magpie appeared in front of me, and with my eyes wide open, I could see him in my garden standing on the grass.

His tail was long and his feathers were black and blue like the sky.

'Good day, Mr Magpie, how are you today?'

'I am fine' he said.

'I need help, Mr Magpie, do you know how to help me? I need some spiritual help.

I have my tablet to make a call but I don't know whom to call or which number to press for some help.

I am not sure about who I am and I don't have superpowers. I heard I will receive a helper.'

Mr Magpie said, 'Hurry up! press 911, and they can help you'

'No, Mr Magpie, that is not the kind of help I need as they don't know anything about Light. There is no crime committed so they can't help me.

Also, there is no victim. Even though, I feel I am the victim because I am so sad. How can I know who am I? Can you help me?

If I don't have superpowers, I can't fly and I can't help my friends to have superpowers so they can fly with me.

What kind of superhero I will be if I don't have powers and I can't fly?'

Suddenly, Mr. Magpie said, 'Don't worry Lucas, I come here to help you. He sent me.'

'Really? This is awesome. I never thought He can help me. Thank you, Mr Magpie.'

At that second, I felt that I recognized His voice from somewhere else, I think I heard Him before. But at that time I was too busy with my tablet to hear Him properly.

I was in a place of confusion, the place was full of noises and I could hardly hear what He was saying.

I tried again, but the noises were louder and louder and his voice was like vanishing. Then I stopped trying to listen to Him and He left.

I know some people will give up spiritual things quickly. But He still send Mr Magpie to help me.

Now I realised I needed to be focused or I won't get what I want.

This time, I made an effort and I opened my ears to hear trying to know what to do.

'Mr. Magpie, please don't go away, I want to listen to your voice, and I want to know what you have to say to me.

Sorry, I should have listened to you but before I couldn't hear you, and I couldn't see you so I didn't believe it. But now I do. I know you are my helper.

Even though, I knew you were always there in my garden. I think I saw you before and I heard your voice but I guess I was too busy.

I have so many questions for you, and I hope you can answer them. Please, I need your help.

My first question is what shall I wear today Mr. Magpie?
I have to hide from my friends or they will recognise me and they will not believe I am a superhero.'

The wind blew, then the sun rose with strength, and its warms rays touched my face.

I heard Mr. Magpie's voice again and he said, 'You should wear black and white like me.

You can be like me today, white in the morning and black at night Like the Yin and Yang, black and white.'

'What? Black and white? But with too much white I can get dirty when I play, and then my tuxedo will be ruined.

And if it is night, and I am half black nobody can see me because there is no light. Oh no, I want to cry; I can't wear a tuxedo.'

Mr Magpie said, 'Why do you want to enter the Word Clouds?'

'No, I don't want to enter the clouds, what is that? What are you talking about Mr. Magpie? '

Then he said, 'Let me explain what Tagxedo is. It is a tool that allows you to make an advanced word –clouds- from the text.'

'You can't understand; I don't want to enter the clouds. Let me explain to you something. A tuxedo is a man's dress jacket, it is also black and white, like me and your feathers.

I want to fly with you so you can show me the world, the skies, Paradise and everything that I dreamt of.
Because I can't see the world with my tablet.

Can you teach me how to fly, please?
I'm worried, what if I can't fly? What if I fall?'

Mr Magpie answered, 'Don't worry, you worry too much, take one day at a time. It will take time to learn, but I can help you.

I just need your full trust in me or it will not work. I know someone that can help you too. Do you want to fly?'

'Yes, Mr Magpie, I want to fly, it was my dream for so long, I always wanted to be a superhero and fly, but I always failed.

49

I tried and it didn't work. But I am ready now, your voice gives me peace and assurance that now I will learn how to fly to Paradise. Please, tell me who is going to help me.

He said, 'There has to be no doubt in your mind, and we need to prepare the way to do it. Your mind has to be free of negative thoughts and old beliefs.

Follow the voice of the spirit world, the guide who will teach you who you are and teach you how to fly to Paradise.'

Suddenly, I heard a sweet voice that said: 'Good day Mr. Magpie, I also want to fly, and I am also black and white.'

And it was Leader my dog, with his floppy ears like an Egyptian god. Maybe he was Cleopatra's dog, the Queen of Egypt.

I was surprised that Leader can talk, and he also wants to fly, that is fantastic!

'I will never leave you, Leader, of course, you can come with me and learn how to fly.'

His tail wiggled, and he was very happy because he wanted to see the world, all that is there beyond his imagination, he wanted to see Paradise. He also wanted superpowers.

This is the best day of my life. I met Mr Magpie who will help me to find Paradise, to know how to fly and I can also bring my dog. I couldn't have done it without Leader.

Then I had a doubt, but Mr. Magpie said that I shouldn't doubt in my mind. I have another question Mr Magpie, 'where are we going?'

He answered, 'To Paradise. You will know the way when you will learn about The Divine. There is a tree and there is a river, you need to know this for now.

Also, many more like us are coming to Paradise and we will see a new world, a New Beginning. That's all you need to know. It will be a specific day, at a specific time and all will know what to do to be in Paradise.

It is like speaking a language, you can't learn in one day, you need to do it step by step, day by day.

So when that day will come many will know what to do to arrive at Paradise. We will all be there at the same time.'

'Thanks, Mr. Magpie for the encouraging words. You are the best. I want to start today; I can't wait.'

Leader said, 'Me too, I am happy to lead the way.'

And he jumped and barked because he was happy.
Then I thought I have another doubt, oh no, I shouldn't doubt. I have another question,

'how much shall I pay you? I don't have a job, so I don't have much money, only some savings, but I can ask my mother to pay you. She wants to come too.'

He answered 'Money? what is money? I don't know what money is. I just want your friendship, a mutual exchange. If I help you then you help me, that is all I need from you.'

'You don't know what money is? It is a piece of paper to buy things like food and clothes that you receive when you work. With some people's faces on it.'

He laughed and then said: 'I don't work but I eat, I don't need money for food. Money doesn't mean anything to me.

51

The Divine is everything to me, He gives me all I need.'

Then I started to think about how to explain to Mr Magpie in another way what money is. And the idea came to me.

'Money is also in coins, have you ever seen these shiny tinny little circles? Some are made of gold, some are silver and some are copper.'

He shouted, 'A cop? Where is the copper, where did you see the police? Run!

Don't talk to the police officer, if you see one copper just don't say anything or you will be charged with a crime.
I have learned that the best way to deal with them is with silence.

They can put in your mouth words that you didn't say, it is called manipulation. I have been arrested only once, and they put me in a cage behind bars.

I didn't do anything. I didn't stop talking because I didn't know that it is better not to talk to them.

When I was in the cage I heard other birds singing and I knew I will come out of there.

I looked for The Divine and peace came to me. He sent someone to help me. I heard a loud voice.

The voice said to me to be still. She said, ' I know that it is not nice to be in a cage. I know you feel oppressed, you can't talk, and the worst of all is that you can't fly and see the world.

I can imagine that there are beautiful places when you know how to fly and see the world. Be still!'

Mr Magpie said, 'As I turned my eyes to see who the voice was, I realised that the voice was coming from a beautiful Magpie.

She was the most beautiful Magpie in this world.

I felt I just knew her. She was dressed like me in a black and white tuxedo. She was like me. She wanted to save me from my cage, that black hole where I felt I was.'

Then, she asked me, 'How can I help you Mr.?'

I answered 'My name is Mr. Magpie. I want to be your friend, but I am in a cage, and I need a little help. Did the Divine send you?'

She answered, 'Yes, He told me you will need help. But I don't have the key to open the cage, and then even if I find the key how can I open the cage?

I must confess that I don't know how to fly very well, I have tried but I failed.'

The story was beautiful and I asked Mr. Magpie to tell me more.

'What did you do that day? I want to know every detail of what happened that day. Did she help you? And did you help her to fly?

Mr Magpie said, 'Of course, she helped me and I helped her. Friends help each other. We all need each other.

I want to go to a place that The Divine showed me in my mind, a magical place, with colours that nobody has ever seen before.

There are many beautiful fruit trees, rivers, and waterfalls, and the sun is always bright, with warm weather all year round, it is Paradise.'

'I also saw that place, I had a dream and it was identical. There were billions of people and animals, and they will come with us to Paradise.

I want to take my friends and my mum there. But the only way to get there is if they all know how to fly. If they know the truth of the Universe.

We can't go by car, by bicycle, by train, or by plane, we only can arrive there if we know how to fly.'

Leader said, 'I want to fly.'

Mr Magpie said, 'Yes, of course, Leader, and I will help you to find who will teach you how to fly and get us to Paradise.'

Now I know I am not just a 'normal' child. I know I will be a hero and I will fly to Paradise. I know that I will have superpowers.

'Thanks, I appreciate your help, Mr. Magpie.'

Then he said, 'Let's go and find some friends.

Let's go! Let's find more friends who want to fly to Paradise.

Chapter 7
The Sceptical Whale

We find someone on our way.

Mr Magpie said, 'Hello, I was here with my friends; Lucas and Leader and we have a plan. We need to learn how to fly to find Paradise.'

The whale said to us, 'Hello, my name is Harry, and I am a whale. How are you going to fly to see Paradise?

Boys and dogs can't fly. They don't have wings. It is impossible.' Then he laughs.

Mr Magpie said, 'What if I told you that someone will teach you how to fly; will you come with us?

Harry laughed again lauder; he blasts into laughter.

Harry said, 'I am a whale I can't fly. Have you ever seen a whale that flies?
I don't think so, that is because they can't fly; whales can only swim.'

Mr Magpie said, 'Maybe you have wrong beliefs, but have you ever tried? I know someone that can teach you.

Your beliefs don't allow you to fly, it is in your mind. When you know about the Spiritual world then you can fly. Simple as that.'

Harry said, 'Really? Do you only need to know and reject your beliefs and then you can fly?'

Mr. Magpie said, 'Harry be still!'

And as Harry was still, we were entering into the same vibration as Mr Magpie.

There was a song that we start singing and was resonating in our minds which made Harry very quiet.

Mr. Magpie said, 'Whales have big brains, the volume of their super-sized brains is 8000 cubic centimetres, which is 5 times more than Lucas' brain.

The whale's brain weighs up to 9 kilograms, almost 20 lbs which is Leader's weight right now. And it is 6 times heavier than Lucas' brain.'

I didn't know this.

'Wow! How do you know all these things, Mr Magpie? '

He answered, 'I know it because I love animals. Do you also like animals, Lucas?'

'Yes, I do.'

Then Mr. Magpie said, 'Do you like to eat animals?'

I didn't answer, I didn't know what to say.

Mr Magpie asked again, 'Do you like to eat animals?'

I didn't answer.

Leader said, 'Yes, he ate fish yesterday.'

Mr Magpie was speaking with a louder voice 'Lucas, did you eat a fish or not yesterday?'

'Well, yes I did eat fish, I am a Pescatarian.'

Mr. Magpie was shocked and said, 'What is a Pescatarian?'

'A Pescatarian is a person who eats vegetarian foods but he is including fish and seafood. Many people are Pescatarians.'

Harry was a bit furious, he was fuming, and he said out loud, 'Lucas, do you eat fish? My friends in the sea are fish. Do you want to eat my friends Lucas?'

I felt sad and confused.

Leader helped me again and answered for me, 'He is not a Pescatarian anymore, is it Lucas?'

I looked astonished at Harry. 'But I like salmon a lot.'

Harry shouted at me, 'Salmon? Salmon is a fish too.'

'Harry was trying to confuse me.

Harry, you eat fish too so why are you judging me?'

I was not sure if I should stop eating salmon or not. I don't want to eat any whale but I still like fish.

Then I said to Harry, 'Ok. Harry I will stop eating fish if you learn how to fly and come with us to Paradise.'

Harry was now nervous and realised that I managed to answer that difficult question and now he was in a problem with my challenge. Harry didn't know what to say.

Then he answered, 'I don't believe I can fly. I can only swim.'

Leader said, 'Come on Harry don't be sceptical! Can you also bring your friend as well, please? and we will all fly to Paradise?'

Then Harry said, 'No, I don't want to believe, there is no Paradise, that is it.'

It is sad, but I knew many will not want to know the truth and I don't want someone like that in Paradise.

I want to find the ones that will desire to know the truth and want to learn to fly. We continued our journey.

Chapter 8

Blessing

Suddenly, as I looked on my left, I saw something but I was not sure if it is an animal. I have never seen something like this before.

I couldn't tell what it was, so I stood up and went toward it.

As I was getting nearer it was looking like a type of horse. At that moment, I heard a noise similar to a horse nicker. I knew that that noise is when horses deeply bond with someone.

But when I got nearer, Leader realised that the animal was not a horse, it was a Unicorn.

'This is impossible, a Unicorn?'

I knew that unicorns were not real; they have never existed. But because I know that in the spiritual world, everything is impossible we could see the unicorn.

I was feeling a bit worried because some things look beautiful but they are in disguise and they trick you with a very good and wise lie.

As I got nearer the unicorn snorted. I knew that they snort when they are happy. I understood that the unicorn was happy to see me and he was welcoming me.

Leader was a bit afraid he didn't know what to do, he stepped backwards. I think he knew something was wrong.

I continued moving forward and petted the unicorn and he did a sighing.

They do this sound when they feel relaxed because I was petting him. I was tempted to ride the unicorn but I decided not to do it.

'Hello, my name is Lucas and I am here with my friends Leader, and Mr. Magpie. I would like to know your name, please.'

I was waiting for him to reply.
At that moment, the unicorn spoke and his voice sounded loud and clear.

He said, 'My name is Love. Today I am a little bit sad because I can't find Blessing.'

'Who is Blessing?'

I didn't know Mr. Magpie was sleeping and when he woke up he saw me talking to the unicorn and walked toward me.

Mr. Magpie said, 'Hello how are you? I am with my friends so that they can learn how to fly. Where is Blessing? We need her to teach them how to fly'

The unicorn said, 'I just woke up some minutes ago and I can't find Blessing. She is very special and very strong.

I am worried, I saw her yesterday we played together, we ate together, and we have fun together but when I woke up this morning she was gone.

I don't understand, I looked everywhere I went up and down the hill but I can't find her.'

'Do you know her? Is she going to help us to be in Paradise? Is she going to help us to fly?'

Love replied, 'Yes, she will. I know her. But I can teach you how to fly, we don't need her.'

Leader sniffs the floor, and he said, 'I can't smell anything. Are you sure she was here?'

I knew that Leader can smell food from very far because that is his superpower but why he can't smell anything here? Was Love telling us the truth?

Love said, 'Yes I am sure, she was here with me.'

'We will find Blessing. We know she will teach us how to fly.'

Chapter 9

Love, Deception and Truth

L ove stopped at the bottom of the hill.

Then he said, 'We were here some days ago with Blessing.

I gave her a rose, she didn't know at first it was me. I hide it near her, she picked it up and then she realised I put the rose there.

She was so happy and I was happy too. It was a multicolour flower; each petal was of a different colour. I created it for her, I manifested it with my power.'

Leader was sniffing and he couldn't feel that this place was full of happiness and joy. He didn't understand why.

Love said, 'I felt great happiness.'

The smell disappeared, it was not there. Her vibration and the energy from her spirit were not here in this place.

We couldn't see her, or feel her presence, her smell, or her happiness. Maybe we should use our spiritual eye.

Love suddenly neigh, this means that he is trying to help himself to calm his separation anxiety because he felt that he was separated from Blessing.

However, we continue our journey until we stopped again at a junction.

Love suddenly remembered something, and he said, 'She was here with me in this same place some days ago. We were both galloping together, that day was a beautiful sunny day.

We spent all day together looking at each other and there was nothing else important but to look into each other's eyes and contemplate each other.

Time was not important, food was not important, the only important thing was to be together and to enjoy the moment.'

Time doesn't exist, it is a man made concept. You can't see time; you use it to measure things.

I know that nature doesn't use a clock or a calculator.

However, nature just knows the exact time for everything. Animals also have an instinct and they also know the perfect time for everything.

For example:

Flowers know when it is daytime and they open their petals and when it is night-time and they closed it.

Animals know when to hunt, sleep, and when they are ready to mate.

All of a sudden, I felt that it was the perfect moment for marvellous things and they will happen soon. I know that everything that is happening is for a good reason and we will know the outcome of it soon.

Leader sniffed again, he could feel the wind in his nose and he felt a strike of energy passing through his nose and body.

Love said, 'She is like a burning fire, full of herself. She used to run wild; she could do anything she wanted.

I remembered what happened that day, she twisted her left leg. She was in so much pain, so I hold her leg.

With my power. she forgot about the pain. I realised that I am stronger than her. She stood up and walked with an amazing smile on her face.

She was healed in that instant because she knew that my power could heal her, she knew the impossible was possible.'

Leader said, 'There is no pain any more in this place but only power. The kind of power that cancels any pain and make things perfect.'

'I think Love is not telling us the truth. I think he wants us to believe that he is more powerful than Blessing.

She knew how to make her pain go away, she was learning her own power in connection with the Divine.'

We had a nap before we continue our journey.

Chapter 10
Question everything

After the nap, when I woke up, I had a dream that Love had lied to us. Everything was a dream.

Love never saw Blessing and now I have realised that it was just a dream and not reality. He told us half-truths so that we deviate from the truth.

He wanted us to follow him so that we can't find the truth. He guided us to lies, fallacies and sophisms.

However, I will focus on the truth.

I think Blessing can hear me and feel our presence as much as I do. I will try to talk to her. 'Blessing can you hear me?'

There was silence, I was trying to hear something. I heard a noise far away.

'I think she can hear me!

I was so happy because if she can hear me then I can communicate through telepathy, and then I will know what she knows and I will be able to be in Paradise.'

Leader said, 'I want to have telepathy too, how do I get it?'

'It is easy. You need to try, that's it!'

Leader said, 'Is that possible?'

'Yes, it is possible when you KNOW that you can do it and you don't have to doubt, not even for a second. It is within you, and depends on what you want and how much you want it.'

Leader said, 'Ok, so I will try it today.'

'It doesn't take too much time to learn it, but the important thing is to know you can do it until one day it will happen when you least expect it.'

Love thought he saw Blessing but she wasn't there. He confessed that it was all a dream.

When we confronted him and asked him questions then we knew the truth. I like to ask questions they always bring me to the truth.

The name of the place was called 'Fulana' then we realised that this is not the place where Blessing was. In Spanish this name has a negative connotation.

Therefore, we realised that Blessing only existed in his mind. He lied about his power, and now we know that she has the power.

All of us need to find her so we can fly. I doubt that his name is Love, maybe he changed his name to confuse us.

I was thinking about what to do next. At that instant, a wind was blowing and, an idea came to me in my mind.
I knew what to do. I have to know what Blessing knows to be in Paradise.

I will question all beliefs and see if I can prove them.

I have to know more...

Chapter 11
Search your Paradise

I knew that all is possible when you know yourself. I wanted to spread my wisdom to all my friends and people and be the happiest I had ever been.

I knew that to do that it will only happen if I will know about Paradise. Therefore, I decided to make Paradise a reality.

It didn't matter how long it will take to find Paradise because, after that moment when I will find it, I will spend eternity there.

Time is not important when you know that you will spend eternity there.

I knew that it will be worth it to search until I will find Paradise. I had to make questions.

I have to live in world, but not be of this materialistic world. It has to be a happy life. I also needed to know how to know this to find Paradise.

I am learning how to have wisdom so that my dream will become true.

There is a secret that you need to know to manifest anything you want. Anything will become a reality.

If it is a secret is because it is hidden and difficult to find.
I have learned how to see with the third eye, the eye of the spirit.

Day by day I was having more wisdom and more questions arise.

Words and meanings of words are important, they can create and manifest anything into a reality. So be careful what you wish.

The Secret to Know Paradise:

Firstly, you have to think about what you want to happen in your life. If you want Paradise, you should focus on that path. Learn different things to arrive at a different path.

Secondly, ask yourself questions and leave the rest to wisdom. Carry that thought from your mind to The Divine.

Finally, the answer will come to you.

However, your mind sometimes may have a negative or wrong thought and it will try to convince you to give up your dream.

Maybe your mind will tell you, 'Don't think about it any more.'
But never give up your dreams or they will never come to pass.

Sometimes your mind will tell you that you don't know everything.

But even if it is true don't worry. You can know what others can't know, just focus. And this will be just because you *knew* that you will understand it.

Your thoughts and your beliefs are not YOU. Search in your dreams, and wait until they will appear.

You also should understand how to keep your mind and thoughts focused and to be patient.

You shouldn't allow any situation to stop your dreams from becoming a reality.

YOU are the creator of your dreams. It is all in your thoughts and your mind.

When you know that your dreams are real nobody and nothing can stop them. Don't stop searching for knowledge and wisdom.

Go for your dreams and don't pay attention to your negative thoughts.

You need to control your thoughts that go to your mind and heart. That's how you will know yourself and Paradise.

You can do it.

But now I needed a plan, I need to find Paradise.

Firstly, I will close my eyes and see with the third eye, not with the physical eyes.

Secondly, I will close my physical ears and listen with my soul.

The dream was already in me, so I needed the eye to make it a reality.

When you understand this, nobody can change or cancel your dreams because you know in them so much that you will never stop until they will happen.

Even if you think that you don't know how to make it happen, it doesn't matter because you will find the way to Paradise. Your soul will remember.

Remember who you are.

Remember your dreams.

Chapter 12
A process of Recollection

Sometimes thoughts can be overwhelming, and negative.

Some people can have evil thoughts and actions.

Negative is not evil. If you have negative thoughts is because there is chaos in your mind.

Evil people are lovers of evil and they are not willing to change.

Love was lying and didn't want to change because he loved being evil.

There is good in life and there is bad. Bad is the absence of good.

The Divine is light, and darkness is the absence of light.

Good people enjoy doing good and bad people enjoy doing bad. There is no middle way.

The body asks for things of this world, for pleasures but the soul asks for the good things of this world.

And everyone has a CHOICE. 'What do you prefer to be?

A body or an eternal soul?

You need to remember and start a process of Recollection.

When I confronted Love and I saw who he was he told me that my dream of flying to Paradise is a fairy tale.

He already decided on which side he wanted to be; the body, the evil side.

His name was not L-o-v-e but E-V-O-L which the spell backwards is 'evil', the deceiver.

He tried to deceive us. I have never seen love, and for me love is perfection. The Divine is love the only and perfect love. The other kind of 'love' is not perfect.

Not everything in life is a lie, there are always some half-truths in everything. You can know this by asking questions. You also can know who is good or bad by their actions not by words.

These evil thoughts were telling Love to lie. They were making him feel that my dreams were not a reality.

He also said that Paradise doesn't exist, that I won't find it. He wanted to destroy my dreams and he wanted to confuse me so I will not know.

He said that he can't get there because he doesn't fly. He wanted me not to have eternal love and he knew that if he can change my thoughts and I doubt I won't see Paradise and I can't find Blessing.

His thoughts were extremely evil and he showed me at the end who he really is. He was very deceptive and through confusion and half-truths, he wanted to take me far from reality.

Reality is what you **know** is real, **a fact** that is logical and undeniable. Nobody should tell you that your reality is impossible because others don't **know** it.

You should ask yourself this:

What is real? What is true?

I know that for everyone what is real or true can be seen in different ways. But we can know lies and truth. Why?

You can see things from a different perspective and these can be positive for you but not for others. Things can be different because we are all different.

No, we are not different, we are ONE. The ones different are the evil entities that want to confuse us.

Don't stop searching for answers and don't stop dreaming, there are no limits to dreams. Fly away with your mind to know the unknown. Don't stop dreaming.

You should realise that your mind could make your day happy or sad. This will depend on what kind of thoughts you have at that moment and what things are you hearing during the day.

These thoughts make you have negative thoughts or sometimes negative feelings. You needed to block these negative thoughts and negative feelings, and the lies that your mind is telling you.

It is very important that you separate yourself from negative and evil people.

Love couldn't convince my mind, he couldn't win. He has to confess that his name was not Love.

He lied to us, but lies don't last long. Therefore, I have to leave him behind. He had a choice and he had chosen the evil side.

To win the battle with your negative thoughts you need to put more attention to your thoughts and start filtering them. Chang the negative thoughts into positive.

Focus on the important things in life, **yourself.**

If your mind says to you that you are sick or you have pain. Then you tell yourself the opposite.

Instead, say this:

'I am not sick and I have no pain, I am not that.'
Even if you feel bad.
These things are permanent but you are not.

'**Just do it, just do it**!'

Don't try to use your brain but use wisdom.

We don't use our entire brain and they don't teach us how to change our negative thoughts. We have to learn it by ourselves.

Nobody teaches this in schools or universities. They don't teach about how to know who you are. They don't teach about the power of the mind or the connection with the Divine.

And only religion has something similar, half-truths. But you don't need a religion to know who you are.

Evil people also know half-truths and use confusion to avoid others to know the truth.

There is power when you **know**.

Good is more powerful than evil.

Search until you will remember everything. Never stop asking questions and never stop searching Paradise.

I spent months perfecting my wisdom, it didn't happen overnight. I had to change many things in my beliefs.

I changed my negative thoughts. Also, I needed to avoid and reject evil people that showed me evil actions. I rejected Love, the fake love.

I changed my thoughts, beliefs and habits that were not helping me to find my destiny. I had to filter and destroy them. I replaced them with new logical facts.

I became very strong and determined and I fought against all evil thoughts. I have won every battle and every ridicule.

Everything I needed to do I achieved it. This was how I learned how to control my thoughts.

Now, there was harmony in my thoughts like the harmony there is in music.

Every note has to be played together simultaneously into a whole unit or composition to produce a pleasant effect.

The frequency has to be at the same time for the music to be in harmony. Because otherwise, it will not be pleasant to the ear.

There is a vertical and horizontal frequency in music that creates harmony. If a frequency can create harmony, you can also create it in your thoughts.

It is a vibration that will be in your mind and will bring positive thoughts and wisdom.

Plants, animals, and people can feel these vibrations of frequencies.

I knew that Blessing's words were like harmony and that she will help me to find Paradise.

When we will be in Paradise it will not be an off-key sound but it will be like the perfect song ever played.

It will be harmony because it will be an unending frequency of peace and love. I have my perfect dream.

I prepared myself for Paradise. I didn't want to use my physical eyes or ears anymore. I wanted to see and hear with the third eye, that's how I will find Blessing and Paradise.

I know that she will bless everyone with her wisdom.

We are ONE in harmony with the same positive thoughts and wisdom.

We don't need to use words to communicate, but telepathy.

Peace and love will reign because many will be ONE Soul.

'Don't try to do it, **just DO IT!**'

I think that our minds will flow in harmony and all of us will hear angels singing and they will speak to us and tell us what to do and where to go.

At the right time, this will happen.

And this is how many will be in Paradise.

If you want to **know** this, search until you will remember who you were, who you are and who you will be.

You will remember that you are a soul that will never die.

Chapter 13
Wisdom and the Right Mindset

The word– <u>I can't</u> - shouldn't exist in our minds. You should never use that word.

Because when you use it, it will have power over you and your thoughts will manifest negativity. You should change that word.

Replace 'I can't' with:

I CAN

<u>Tell to yourself:</u>

'I cando everything.

I can do everything I put my mind on. Wisdom is within me and anything is possible for me.

The Divine is within me with his power and is helping me'

This should be your *new mindset*.

Wisdom and knowledge are not the same.

<u>*Knowledge*</u> is something you learn, study, read, or you know by experience.

You can't learn wisdom from a book.
You just know it by opening your third eye and communicating with the ONE.
Also, you will gain good judgment.

You need to consider the consequences of your decisions, and you should think before acting and speaking.

In this way, your life will be greater and easier because you will know always what to do.

When you will understand this concept, you will want to get hold of wisdom for a better life.

Wisdom comes only from *the Divine* who knows everything.

To communicate with the spiritual world, you need to desire to do it and know how to do it. You need to understand that there is a connection to make, and the way is with the third eye.

It is not by knowledge but it is by wisdom that you get there. It is not by not having any thought or meditating, nor by doing something.

You need to remember this is the process of Recollection.

Knowledge can be a first step, but it has to be a different knowledge. Before that, you need to empty the previous beliefs and ideas and then you can fill your mind with new ones.

Suddenly, I entered into a deep vision. I saw a heart made of gold, and I knew the meaning of my vision. The meaning was that Blessing had her heart made of gold.

This reminded me of the verse that said:

PR.16:16 'BUT HOW MUCH BETTER IS IT TO GET WISDOM THAN GOLD, TO GET INSIGHT RATHER THAN SILVER?'

This parable made me understand that wisdom is very important and we need to desire to have it.

When you have wisdom you can know how to get anything in life. There will be nothing you will not know how to do or how to overcome.

I was now in search of more wisdom to find my dream. I had to know things from the spiritual world so that I can fly.

If you want to get something different that you couldn't get before you need to do something different to get it.

However, many people chose the easy way, that is to continue living without making anything different in their lives.

Doing it this way won't bring any solution to your problems but the same old outcomes.

Having your old beliefs and doing the same things as always and living in the same way, won't bring any changes.

But if you want a different outcome you need to think in a different way to have different ideas that can bring you to a breakthrough.

These can be your negative thoughts before you decide to change your mindset:
What if I can't change my beliefs? What if Paradise doesn't exist? What if I can't fly?

Then your positive thoughts should be these:
I know I will find the wisdom and I will be in Paradise, I can experience it and I know it does exist. I will know how to fly.

Then the negative thoughts may appear again because there was a little doubt. Or because you didn't try harder to practice this positive mindset.

You needed to remove negative thoughts, beliefs and negative people around you.

Maybe your negative mind will say:
What if I can't fly or maybe I don't understand how to do it? I'm suffocating just thinking about this, I need a solution.

Maybe I need perfection in me but I am not perfect, I'm far from being perfect. What if I say that everything is possible and then I can't change? Then maybe it won't happen.

I was fighting my negative mindset too and I know how hard it can be at the beginning.

But you should tell yourself:
I am strong, I can do anything. My soul/spirit is perfect to know what to do. I will experience miracles. The impossible will be possible for me. I will see it with my eye.

I will learn who I am, I love myself, and I will be able to do the impossible. I can move mountains. I can change a problem and create a solution.

I can create what is not there and make it real. The power is within me. The Divine spirit is within me.

After knowing this and the way to manifest Paradise, I felt an aura around me.

I could see the power manifesting; this is the power I was talking about.

I know that I will see Paradise and that I will make my dream come true. I will be a superhero with superpowers.

You can have the same powers too.

I was experiencing power because even words are power. It was not difficult because I had no doubt.

I CAN do it, I CAN think positive, I will do it. I CAN do all things. I will turn these thoughts into positive ones.

I'm confident, and I know deep in my heart that I CAN do everything. *Absolutely everything!* The Divine is within me.

I have learned how to turn negative thoughts into positive thoughts. I have changed my mindset, and fear disappeared. I have no doubts, and I knew my power. I know who I am.

This is the way to Paradise. It is only for those who can **know**, **remember**, and have **wisdom** without a minimum of doubt.

The ones that know themselves and their power will know the Divine, the ONE.

I know Blessing has self-esteem and she is confident, she knows when to talk and what to say. She also had to learn how to change her mindset. She needed knowledge.

She had learned how to fly. She is already in Paradise waiting for us.

She remembered and learned how to be in this peaceful place that we want to be. She wanted so much to be there and to know how to fly and she tried until she made it.

But she also wants us to be there.

She searched for wisdom from the Divine and she knew herself.

Also, she knew the power within her. And that power revealed to her all the secrets that she needed to know about Paradise.

When YOU will **know** who you are, you will find that power and Paradise.

When you will have wisdom you will **know** things you didn't know existed before.

When you will learn how to manifest Paradise and create it within yourself then you will be with us.

Are you willing to change?

Contemplate new knowledge to remember.

Paradise is the eternal place for eternal minds with eternal love, peace, and happiness.

Chapter 14
On our way to Paradise

We all want to fly and find Blessing so that she will help us to be in Paradise.

On our way, we saw ***the Ram***. He has an arrogant sense of leadership and determination. He may help us to gather the right team to fly to the other side.

The ram may help us because he can fight with his red and yellow horns. His actions can be decisive. It is an important task.

He was not ready to answer his call to go to Paradise. He is inexorable. As a ram, he is very proud of himself, he didn't want to be the second in command.

Besides, he wants to do everything the way he wants as a Narcissist.

He said, 'Do you really think you are the boss? Who do you think you are? You know nothing about dreams.
Also, I don't follow false prophets but laws.'

'You are too rude. I also follow the Law. The Natural Law.'

He asked me, 'What is Natural Law?

'I am not surprised that you don't know what it is as it's the only Law.

Natural law, according to St. Thomas Aquinas: "The light of reason is placed by nature- and thus by God- in every man to guide him in his acts.

Therefore, human beings alone among God's creatures, use reason to lead their lives." This is Natural Law.' (www.crf-usa.org)

I will explain what this means for you. This means that deep inside of you, you know what is right and what is wrong.

We don't need anyone to tell us or show us this. Even if you are born in the jungle you can know this law.

Do no harm, no injury, and no loss. That is enough. These three words mean the same, do nothing bad to anyone or anything.'

The ram said, 'Do you want to laugh at me, ridicule me?
You don't know this; you just want to fake that you are good but now I know you don't. So better go away from me.'

I didn't answer because there was no point to argue with him. He doesn't know what is right. I know that it is difficult to know the spiritual world.

But that is the only way to Paradise. Only those who desire and yearn for justice will be there.

The ram is arrogant, rude and narcissistic like the unicorn Love. However, his name was Evil, not Love. He deceived and lied to us.

Unfortunately, some people will never come to Paradise.

Because they will never desire and search for wisdom.

They are sceptical, pessimistic and prefer to believe what they can see.

They think they know everything and they don't want to change their beliefs.

∞ ∞ ∞

The next morning, we met ***the Bull***.

He is bull-headed, he is perseverant, and a loyal friend. He will be taking us through our spiritual world, seeing beyond the physical world into the cosmic light of Paradise.

'How are you? Do you want to come with us? We need to find Blessing and with her, we will all fly to Paradise.'

The bull said, 'Hello. I don't know If I can, I am too old and heavy for this, I need to think about it. I am afraid of new things. I always believed what I see and I am not so sure.'

'We want you with us, we need your strength and knowledge. I know you will know what to do to find her and when you will see her you will understand everything.

I know that everything will be fine because you have a beautiful heart.

Even though you are tough and strong from the outside, I know you can fly to the other side. You just need to relax.

We will all experience the same kind of power but you need to believe that we will go to Paradise.

You need wisdom, let go of negativity and doubt.'

The bull said, 'I know that what you are saying is right, I am positive and I have no doubt now about this. I will see Paradise; I will follow all of you. Let's do it!'

'Thanks, let's go.'

As we continue walking we met two butterflies. They were there waiting for us.

∞ ∞ ∞

I just knew they are supernatural, ambivalent ***butterflies***.

The mortal and immortal twins can't be separated because they are one.

You compare them with a coin that has two sides. But it is still ONE coin. They can be different but are part of the whole.

They are fundamentally opposite. Good and bad. Hate and love. You need to know one to know the other. You can't know what love is if you never experience hate.

You can't know what is good if you never experience what is evil. You need to know what is darkness to know what is Light. By making mistakes, you learn what is good.

Besides, to know which is the right choice you need always to have more than *two* choices. We can't choose if we have only *one* option.

Therefore, only when there are more than two options we can then think and decide which one to choose. Especially if we have to go through new places to find the ultimate path we need to know which one is the right one.

The butterfly that didn't want to change her mindset said,

'Why do all of you want to do this? I think you are all full of illusions and you will be deceived. You don't know where Blessing is or if you can find her.

I don't want to judge you but I think it is a bit extreme, you are believing in dreams. They are impossible!'

The positive butterfly said, 'Why you can't believe them? Sometimes things are not what they look like. You need to see things differently.

Things that are related to the spiritual world must not be seen as 'normal' because they are not.

You need to learn about wisdom to understand the unknown.

Then, you will know the spiritual world. Many can't see it because they are focused on the things they see with their physical eyes or half-truths. They need to open the third eye.

I love you so much, but you are wrong and you are still with your old mindset. Raise your vibration and you will see with the third eye.

This is the eye of the impossible, and then it will be possible.

You need to leave aside many beliefs that will make you go away from the right path. You need a new mindset. Positive thoughts, wisdom, no fear and no doubts.'

The negative butterfly answered,

'Well, maybe or maybe not. I like who I am and what I believe and I don't intend to change a bit! It is too hard to change and I don't see the point. I like the way I think and what I believe.

I only know this way of thinking and I don't know another one. Why should I change? Why do I have to believe in something I can't see or understand?'

The positive butterfly answered, 'Do you want to go to Paradise? If your answer is yes, then you need to do something now, don't wait because it can be too late.

You should look around you and realise that there is a perfect world.

There is perfection in nature and your soul, what is not perfect is what you see with your physical eyes.

Animals and plants always have food, water and shelter.
I have decided I want to go. And what about you?'

She was quiet for a while, she looked around and then said,

'Yes you are right nature is perfect like our souls. I will come; I want to believe in Paradise. Even if I think it is hard I will search for wisdom and I will change. I will reset my mind.'

I was so pleased she put in the effort to change and she will achieve it.

$$\infty \infty \infty$$

We follow the path and we met ***the crab***.

She can adapt to water and land. She will represent mother earth with her deep power of creation. She is loyal among friends with her bonding power and strength.

I asked her, 'Do you want to come with us? We are going to fly, we will find Blessing and we will be in Paradise.'

She said, 'I would love to come with all of you, but I am so busy. I have a busy life. I have many things to do and right now I think I am not in the right mindset.'

'I am Lucas; I know it is difficult sometimes. Things can move forward and sometimes backwards. However, I promise you this is not just a dream; it will come to pass, it's a prophecy.'

She said, 'Yes, but I don't have time and it's difficult and hard to find wisdom. It is difficult for me to leave my family and go with you. Because they don't believe in Paradise.

Do you really believe we can fly and be in Paradise? I am very comfortable here where I am. I have my friends and my family but I would like to be in Paradise too. I don't know what to do!'

'You can always find time for wisdom because it is the most important thing to change your life forever.
We will fly and then we will be in Paradise.

Please think again.
Do you really want to miss this opportunity?

What if is the only opportunity you have?

Sometimes things happen only once in a lifetime and you need to achieve them at the right time or they are gone. And this is your life, your family can't decide for you.'

She thought for a moment and then she said,
'ok, I am coming too.'

'Great, she is coming, I am very happy.'

A new day, a New Beginning has started, and I was thinking about who else will be in Paradise.

∞ ∞ ∞

I met the lion, the magnificent**_Lion_**.

The power is within his soul. It will be nice to have him on the journey to find Blessing. He can help us to know the deepest wisdom so that we can find Paradise.

'I need to talk to you Mr. Lion, do you know about my dream? Now is the right time to find Blessing and I know you can help us. I saw it in my dream that you will help us to find her.'

The lion said, 'Ciao, come stai? How are you? I was in the jungle today thinking about Paradise. Then, I had a dream about it.'

'I had to Know myself first and then I had to change my mindset and now it is the right time. I have learned it.'

The lion then said, 'It is exactly what I was thinking when I had the dream. In my mind, some words were resonating within me. I heard these words:

The seeds are ready to germinate. Then, when I looked at the sun, I realised it is in the right position, and soon the harvest is ready.

I saw many beautiful jasmine flowers around Blessing. I saw the sun shining on her face, and I saw her in adoration following her heart, she was already in Paradise.'

'Thanks, that is what I needed to hear, my heart is glowing and expanding with the most beautiful feeling of completion.

I am so happy we will see her and we will fly to Paradise.

∞∞∞

On the way, we saw ***the bee***.

The dream became more clear to me. What the lion said about the harvest was making more sense now.

When the bee appeared, then I knew the harvest was ready. Because he is the divine symbol of diligence, carefulness, and persistence in any work.

He also has the seven heavenly virtues: faith, hope, love, fortitude, justice, temperance, and prudence.

His emblem is abundance and fruitfulness for the journey.

He said he never sleeps; because this is the time to be awake so that we have control of our minds to harvest from our labour.

Who has wisdom will harvest.

REV.14:18 SAYS, 'THE HARVEST OF THE EARTH IS RIPE.'

The lion was right. I need your sweet honey and virtues. I need this honey to be very sweet so that in times of trouble we can have some power from your special honey. And we will receive these virtues.'

The bee said, 'I know how to do it, I will pour in the honey for all of you. Take this honey, it is for everyone that wants to feel the peace of Paradise.

And this will bring eternal, everlasting, and unfailing peace.

That peace will be unbreakable and indestructible. A kind of peace that you never experience before. You need to understand it and it will happen.

That peace will transform any problem into power.

With this power, we will all be the healers of the world. Blessing will bless all of us. She will also be our medicine when she will pour the oil that will never end. She will pour and pour oil and she will harvest and harvest.

Healing and power will be within her for the world to recognise that all is possible when you know your power.

Because she knew this many will **know** it too. The ones that will come with us will be her harvest.'

I am amazed at these words, they gave me the strength to continue with the search for more wisdom, thank you, my friend.

After some days, we met *the swan*.

She will be like a scale. She knows how to break through. She has clairvoyance.

She is the beauty, purity, and kindness that will help us to find the angel's help. She can talk to angels.

She brings transformation, empowering of your mind, and communication with the spiritual world.

'Hello, do we need angel's wings to fly to Paradise?'

The swan said, 'No, we don't need real wings. I know we will find Blessing because the angels told me that all of us will have also spiritual wings to fly high.

The time is near; the time is now. Always follow your heart because your heart is open knowing what to do. Do not give up, Blessing is near I can feel it.'

I was so excited and I had a lot of knowledge and wisdom, I can't wait to be in Paradise.

The next day, we saw ***the eagle.***

He represents Recollection to know who we were and who we are. She will make us remember everything.

Therefore, we will be renewed, awakened, changed, and transformed to start a new life, *a new beginning.*

The eagle said, 'I had a dream about Blessing being in a cage but I saw also that we were opening that cage. This dream means that she was renewed and she had a new life, a *new beginning*.

She has changed, all her powers are ready for the great transfiguration.

I will prepare the fire and I will burn some incense, all is ready now. We will be in Paradise. I saw in my dream that billions will come with us too.

The dream will come to pass and nobody can stop it or I will tear them with my hook beak. Victory is assured.

Those who know their power through wisdom will be there with us.'

We continue our journey.

∞ ∞ ∞

Suddenly, we met ___*the Centaur.*___

He showed his great power. He can build a spiritual bridge between Earth and Paradise.

With his bow and arrow, he can defend us from any wrong mindset. He is the seer and prophet with the power to guide us to the truth.

The truth can be known only if you have wisdom and if you are tuned with the Divine. You can only enter Paradise with a pure mind and heart.

He can use all his horsepower to overcome adversity.

The Centaur said, 'I will defend all of you against those who won't allow us to go to Paradise.

I will build the spiritual bridge that will make anyone believe and know the impossible is possible.

I will protect your minds from negative and evil thoughts. Nothing can defeat us. I am strong and with the ability of my bow and arrow, I will never miss the target.

I will change any old mindset to a new one. I have been training in the wilderness with the fierce beast and I have always won.

I have a steel armour and with it I am unstoppable.'

I was amazed, he is a mighty warrior.

'Please, if there is any problem when you hear the sound of the trumpets move forward.

I can see in my dream that billions will follow us on this path after the sound of the trumpets.

Together we will do everything we need to achieve the transfiguration, and we will have a *new beginning*.'

The Centaur said, 'I saw in my dream that many are following us, and they will know the way at the right time.

Like Moses' story; we will cross to the other side, to the <u>promised land,</u> that is our Paradise. It will be when we are all ready.'

'You are right Paradise is the promised land, and I also know that many will be there.

You need to cross from the old mindset of wrong beliefs to the new mindset.

You need to know that the Divine and the angels are helping us.

When you know, you know. Nobody can take it from you.'

∞ ∞ ∞

We continue walking and then we met ***the goat***.

He wants to come with us as well. With his confidence, he can go to the top of the hills, and he can arrive at the end of any rocky situation with determination.

Also, with only two inches of space, he can climb a mountain and gain a solid step. Because of his determination, he can be strong in any difficult situation and circumstances.

The goat said, 'Hola amigos! I have climbed the highest mountains and I have experienced some of the most difficult situations.

I will come with you to give you the strength to overcome any conflict and overcome the fears that may be in your old mindset.

Fear nothing, and search for wisdom so that everything is possible. It is even possible to fly.
Vuela! Fly with your mind, you can do it.'

'I am happy that you will be with us, but that's why we need friends, to push us in difficult situations.

Shoulder to shoulder we will win anything and we will arrive at the destination.

Even if it takes us a while, nothing will stop us, mi amigo. Gracias, thank you, I appreciate it. We all need each other.

I am so happy to have friends like you who understand me and want to be in the same frequency and vibration.

The only frequency that makes you alive is –the love frequency.'-

∞ ∞ ∞

94

As soon as I turned around, I saw ***the rabbit***.

He is all-knowing. His psychic powers along with an escape plan make him an artist in this subject.

The rabbit said, 'I am ready for an escape plan if we will be in trouble. We need a meeting place where to discuss our plans. Let's go to the caves.

You need to understand that all is already written. We will find a way to connect with Blessing and we will have all our powers joined together.

I know that she found wisdom from the Divine who told her how to escape her deepest difficult thoughts that wanted to prevent her to be at peace.

But, this is the year and the time that she arrived at the transfiguration.

We are in the Age of Aquarius, and it is time we will know everything.

That means the Divine is connecting with us in dreams and visions to reveal to us things we didn't know before.

We will have wisdom; the wisdom we didn't have before.

We will know, what we couldn't know before.

We will transfigure into power to overcome anything.'

'Thanks, that is exactly what I had in my thoughts. Peace and love will reign forever. Not only for us but for many in this world.'

Last but not least, we met ***the dolphin***.

She has sensitivity, deep awareness, faith, endurance, and serenity. She is the essence of life, the water in the universal realm.

Without water, there is no life. She can depressurize gravity so we can fly. She has powerful communication skills. With her, we can find our *new beginning*.

She can break any barrier of the unknown with vibrations so that whatever you think will become true. You shouldn't worry.

'THE LAST WILL BE THE FIRST, THE FIRST LAST; FOR MANY WILL BE CALLED, BUT FEW CHOSEN.' MATTHEW 20:16

The dolphin said, 'Last night, I had a dream and I heard someone singing a song. I think it might be Blessing. She was standing, singing a beautiful song.

I didn't understand at first who was singing it. But then, suddenly, all was clear and I heard the most amazing melody.

While she was singing I understood it was a calling for an awakening for the whole world to wake up. I felt she is connected with all of us and she is trying to communicate with the world.

Whoever listens to this song will come to Paradise.'

'She was right, I know that dolphins use a method called echolocation, which means that they can detect their surroundings to find food, navigate, identify other species, and avoid obstacles.

Dolphins have an amazing setup for hearing sounds. Sound and Light are the attributes; they are disturbances in the Aether.

'LIGHT IS A LONGITUDINAL DISTURBANCE IN THE AETHER.' (KEN WHEELER)

'LIGHT IS A "SOUND" WAVE IN THE AETHER.' (NIKOLA TESLA)

The dolphin was singing the same song Blessing was singing.

I was very interested in this subject so I gather a lot of information to know how to understand Nature.

I wanted to know as much as I can to arrive in Paradise and have a *new beginning.*

Now we had a lot of knowledge and wisdom and many friends that want to start the transfiguration.

My convictions were growing day by day, and I knew the right time to step out was right now, at this specific moment.

We will find Blessing. I called all my friends and said to them that everything is ready to continue our journey.'

Chapter 15
Power

I have power, I know I can do anything. I have learned that I can manifest whatever I want. I know myself and my power.

I know that this power is coming from the Source, The Divine.

It is not coming from 'nothing', because nothing will manifest nothing at all. This is the most important lesson I have learned.

I know I am confident and I know I am powerful; that's how I know I will find Paradise no matter what.

If I wouldn't have seen Paradise in my dreams, I wouldn't have understood that I needed to be there.

I liked how I was. But I needed to change for me, my mum, and my friends. I wanted to fly so I can show them that they can do it and we can go to Paradise.

You can't know there is a Paradise until you see it. You can't know that life is imperfect until you see perfection. Only then, you can understand.

I had to close my physical eyes to find The Divine and Paradise. I had to change my mindset and I had to have determination.

I have to be resilient and fight my wrong mindset. I never gave up. I know I will be in Paradise I saw it in my dreams. I can't wait for that moment to happen.

When you fully know the truth no one can change your mindset.

I know myself. I know that nothing will move me, nothing can change me. No chains can restrain me; no one can change me.

I am powerful and if I fall I rise again until I arrive at 'Home' 'Paradise'.

Even if I am in a big problem, I will come out triumphant in any situation. Because I was made to fight and overcome anything for the future I am destined to.

Paradise is my final destination, and many will come with us.

I will also help others to arrive at this wonderful Paradise. That is my end goal. It is the best place to be, nothing can be better than that place. It is here on Earth.

Paradise is a peaceful place made of love. There is joy, it is eternal, and without pain or sickness. It is a place where you won't lack anything, and we will have intense peace for everyone.

We will be together being loved, sharing everything, and in peace. Love makes things perfect.

That place is in your mind and will be manifested on earth when you will have wisdom. When you will see with your third eye. When you will want to know about The Divine.

You will know what to do. These are not just words. Action is coming. Words can deceive but actions can't.

That is why you need to learn how to control all your senses. You shouldn't use your eyes or your ears. You should use your third eye to see who you really are and where you belong to.

You will never be confused; you will never be manipulated by any force or any lie in y mind. And when you will have the same state of mind, you will be in Paradise.

Remember, the Power is within you and it will be manifested. You should ask yourself questions to know who you are.

When you become your own masters and you know yourself then you will know that nobody owns you.

You will know that there is nobody more powerful than The Divine within you, because you are like Him, and we are all spirit.
That is how you will see Paradise with the third eye.
We are all ONE.

We are One vibratory energy that manifests anything.

We are the Power of this World.

You are the Light that can't be switched off.

You have the Power of the Divine within you.

Chapter 16

Blessing's Liberation

I have spoken telepathically with Blessing and she is telling me how she learned the truth of Liberation.

She said, 'One day, I was feeling that something very good will happen to me soon.'

Several times she woke up in dreams and visions saying things that pertain to the future. She could see Paradise, and she needed to get out and find it at all costs.

Blessings was asking questions to many people but this was confusing her because there were many different opinions.

Therefore, she realised that she needed to find her own truth by herself but she needed wisdom from the Divine.

She will never give up her dream because she knew in her heart that everything will become reality sooner or later.

One day, many will know and realise that she always spoke the truth.

She will only think about how to find Paradise. She also knew that she has to change her mindset to find Paradise.

At the right time, she decided to change her life and leave every negative person and thought behind and she did it.

She has to leave behind evil family and friends or she won't arrive at her destination.

She was determined, she knew that it was what she needed to do and that nothing will stop her.

However, she knew that not only she will find Paradise, but others will find it too.

Many will also know what she knows and they will be the ones who will live in harmony in Paradise with the same mindset.

She always knew that her destiny was amazing, she always saw herself in a place full of peace and love. It was like in a fairy tale, surrounded by others that know the same.

Who told you that the word 'fairy tale' means that it is something unreal? Who made you believe this?

Now it is time to change it. *'Un-learn'* what they taught you.

She never worried too much about what others said about her or what others think about her dreams. She knew her dreams were REAL, and that they will come to pass.

Her heart never doubted that it will become reality and that it wasn't a fairy tale. She kept her mind positive and she didn't allow others to change her mindset and truth.

When you know something a hundred per cent, nothing can change it.

She always felt like Cinderella, living in a world where sometimes good people will be in pain and sorrow.

This world is full of suffering, injustice, pain, and especially without love.

She wants to help to save and heal this world. She wants to have the power to do it. But she needed to save and heal herself first.

She felt that one day that power will come to her and she will be transformed to arrive to Paradise.

Then, all the world will be as perfect as her fairy tale. She knows that it can only happen to those who can *know* the **Absolute Truth**.

She knew that others can do it if she can do it. *Wisdom* will change the world into a beautiful place full of love and peace forever.

She was unstoppable now and full of wisdom and truth.
You need to be like her with the same wisdom.

You need to know the unknown so that you will understand that what you see is not the *Absolute Truth*.

She wants you to have the same wisdom as her.

Chapter 17
Fairy tales are Real

I think everybody once in a lifetime will dream of Paradise but some will choose to forget about it or not to believe in it.

Blessing's story was similar to the one of Cinderella. Because they didn't tell both of them that there was another world outside the world they knew.

Their 'real' world was not a good place.

The other world the 'fairy' tale world was wonderful, powerful, and perfect.

Nobody told Cinderella that if you have dreams they can become real.

Nobody told her you should have wisdom that is hidden to find the 'real' world.

She only knew a world of poverty, anger, jealousy, lies, abuse of power, sadness, pain, and injustice.

She was forced to be a servant and she was washing clothes and cleaning the house. She was a slave of her work.

She didn't know that she was not born to be a servant but she was born to be free when she will find the truth and wisdom.

Nevertheless, what changed and saved her life was that she spent a lot of time with nature and with animals. Animals are spiritual guides.

Her heart was good and she learned how to make herself happy in every situation. Besides, she started to learn how to talk to the animals and that made her very happy.

Cinderella was not alone anymore; she did all her chores with happiness.

She saw another side of life, she realised that in bad situations you can make yourself happy with what you have and with whom is around you.

However, that was not enough. She believed that animals can talk, and she had her first dream come true.

In addition, she started singing and that made her happier. The song's vibration was the way she could dream.

She started thinking about the unknown, miracles and dreams.

The animals started to talk to her and they helped her.

Due to this miracle that was a fact, she started to know that everything is possible. She wanted to know this power so that she can see a perfect place.

She was creating her Paradise.

At that moment when she felt that there was hope, she started to see that place in her mind.

This was the knowledge that they have been hiding from her.

She understood the Power and with it, she was creating her Paradise.

However, she couldn't see it before because they lied to her. They wanted her to believe that she will always be a slave.

She couldn't see the place because they show her that only this life was reality. They said that only what you see is real.

They told her that she doesn't have to believe in the impossible because that is a fairy tale and doesn't have logic.

They told her to follow orders and commands from other people superior to her.

Nevertheless, she started to understand that nobody is superior. That you can see perfection in nature and in human bodies.

She was thinking and asking herself questions. She realised that we are all equal, we are all free. They didn't tell her that.

They made her believe that she needed to follow rules so she doesn't hurt herself or others. But she realised that to be controlled is not freedom.

She realised that not only evil exists but perfection too. Therefore, she started thinking where is this perfection coming from?

How do you make perfect things and who is creating them? She didn't have the answers yet.

When she realised that she was free and that she can believe and know whatever she wanted, she felt at peace. It was like being in Paradise.

Suddenly, the animals told her about the fairy godmothers.

As soon as she saw that animals can talk she knew that everything was possible. They visited her and clothed her with a dream dress.

That dress was manifested because she knew there is a better world.

The dress was her first connection with the spiritual world and with the impossible.

After that, she saw it with her eyes, and she understood that there was another reality when she was glowing in her fairy tale dress.

But if she didn't known about this world, then it wouldn't have happened.

Besides, she realised that those animals showed her the truth, and this reality was a fact and set her free of her old beliefs.

They told her to believe in dreams which are the **Absolute Reality.**

Now she had facts and she could find her destiny. She decided to go for her destiny, so she started to run without wasting any more time.

Because she changed her mindset, she was no longer in that evil and wrong reality but she was in her beautiful and new reality.

Her third eye opened, and without waiting any longer, she ran as fast as she could. Nobody could help her.

She needed to know things by herself. Nobody can learn and decide things for you.

You need to learn how to know them by yourself. Because if you need someone to save you from this ignorance, that is not to be free and powerful.

Instead, this is being controlled so they can tell you what to believe and what to think.

However, there are 'spiritual helpers' that can teach you to grow in knowledge and wisdom.

It is important to learn about this power to overcome this world to arrive to Paradise, the 'Fairy tale' world.

You can do it.
Cinderella did it and Blessing did it too.

At that moment, Cinderella's great desire materialised, it was not a dream it was now a reality.

She danced with her Prince and it was perfect.
She felt she was in Paradise.

Unfortunately, she couldn't control her fear because everything was so perfect and beautiful that she started doubting.

That feeling of fear was coming from negative thoughts because they told her that perfection doesn't exist.

A negative thought started in her mind. And because of that negative thought, everything changed abruptly.

She couldn't transform that thought into a positive one because fear was more powerful.

Doubt brought fear in her because her mind was full of wrong beliefs. They told her that perfection doesn't exist.

Her negative beliefs made her think that this beautiful moment and the Prince were all a fairy tale story.

They told her that fairy tales don't exist and are not real.

The thought become stronger and she felt that everything was not real.

Her mind was confused, she remembered that at noon everything will end.

Time scared her. Why did she think about time? Because they told her that time exists, even though, you can't see time. When she looked at the clock, time was ticking.

She felt stressed and she forgot to relax and change that negative thought into a positive one.

Why did she believe lies? Because she was confused, she trust they were telling her the truth. They confused her mind with half-truths and lies. She was having a cognitive dissonance after knowing this.

She made a mistake, but she needed to learn from the mistake. She shouldn't be afraid. Fear block her mind and she couldn't think straight.

Also, she looked at her past life and she forgot about her present one.

In that past life, she was sad. They told her that perfection and fairy tales are not real.

They also said that she shouldn't believe in fairy tales. Her mind played a trick on her. She didn't use the third eye and she went away from her perfect destiny.

At that point, she doubted reality and because of that, she was afraid.

Doubt is **fear, fear** is **doubt**.

Fear paralysed her, and she became a slave again. That is how they controlled her.

Unfortunately, she went to her past life; she was in a trap again. She had negative thoughts and she had no more hope of a perfect future. She was confused and depressed.

Cinderella ran because she was scared and she knew that she will return to her slave life. She thought that her house was a safe place and changing her beliefs was difficult.

Nonetheless, changes are opportunities to become better, and also, to have knowledge and understanding. She had to change her old beliefs and learn new ones but it was not easy.

Who taught her not to believe in perfection and not to believe in dreams? Who taught her that big dreams can't become reality even if they seem impossible to her eyes?

However, fear and doubt can destroy your future possibilities. She chose what seemed easier for her but in the end, it was the wrong decision.

There is no freedom in fear. But there is freedom in new things, new possibilities and wisdom.

Fortunately, on her way back to her old life, she lost one of her shoes.

The Price picked it up.
She held on to the other one.

However, she was lost in fear and she needed to learn how to overcome fear, or she will never see him again and she will be a slave forever in that house.

That little shoe was the only thing the Prince had left from that angelical encounter and that supernatural reality.

It was what kept them united in hope.
He went to look for her and he find her to complete their destiny together.

He never gave up, he knew it was real and that everything is possible.

He searched for her, he grew in knowledge and wisdom to find her.

It is difficult to wait for your destiny to arrive. Sometimes it takes longer than expected. It seems like a dream but you know it's not.

Sometimes, it may seem that it is not going to happen. Especially, when it's about the unknown and seems impossible to believe or to see.

But there is always something that connects you with the spiritual world, something that will remind you that it is not just a dream and that is going to happen.

The connection is your third eye and in her case the shoe.

Cinderella was left with only one shoe which was her proof that what happened that day was true.

However, she believed in this reality because she saw the evidence that perfection also exists in nature.

Also, the shoe was the proof that this wonderful new world was real.

Both decided to search and find their perfect world.
The Prince was searching for her, and he found her.

When he put the shoe on her, their fairy tale became real.

The world that before was violent, hostile, and full of fear and lies, became the unreal world.

The fairy tale became the real world. After their encounter the world changed and it was perfect.

That little shoe kept him connected. That thought was enough to keep waiting to see her again because he knew that it will be manifested into a reality.

They believed and knew perfection. They saw their perfect reality.

Everything was predestined, it was written. Because of this wonderful eternal encounter, they lived and know things that they had never imagined before.

Destiny can't be changed and because they knew that there is a *New Beginning* with a new life of peace and love this reality existed for them.

That shoe was the memory of that incredible and divine reality that she saw in her dreams. She waited for this reality her whole life because it was in her thoughts and heart.

She **remembered** that she saw this perfect world in her mind before.

The 'real' world was exactly what oppressed her, made her suffer, and confuse her. So that you don't think about the fairy tale world.

In the 'real' world people will tell you that you need to fit in. To be 'normal' and to follow rules that sometimes don't have any sense.

These rules are made to tell you what to do, what to believe, what to answer and what to think. And if you don't do as you are told, then you are the odd and the rebel one, and they will reject your revolutionary ideas.

They will label you.

But in the 'dream' world, there is power and it is real.

Her 'dream world' seemed impossible. Because all her life she was living in that negative reality with much suffering and disappointment.

Because of this, she couldn't imagine a different reality with a perfect world.

But Cinderella's heart was on fire like Blessing's one. That divine reality of Paradise was alive in her mind too.

After this, she decided to leave all her fears behind. Fears are from your negative past experiences or negative thoughts of the future.

Fear can come when you realise that almost everything that they taught you is not the complete and absolute truth.

However, there is no fear when you have wisdom.

Blessing understood this and she changed her mindset and stop her fears.

She could only do this when she wanted to follow her destiny without thinking about her past beliefs. Then, she was able to change them and she had no more fear.

Then, her dreams became reality.

The day she knew and understood how to arrive at her perfect destiny, she found Paradise.

Finally, Cinderella lived happily ever after without fear but with wisdom.

Cinderella' story taught me that we are on this earth to learn how to make this earth Paradise.

You have to learn to be able to live in the way you should live, in peace and love.

Before you find Paradise you need to search wisdom. Wisdom is logical and real, with real facts.

You have the power to transform this world into Paradise with 'the third eye' and connect with the Divine.

You need to learn about the unseen, that the impossible is possible and that the reality you see with your eyes is not the ultimate reality.

You need to see the other reality, the one you can see with your 'eye' and it will be manifested.

The Divine has always been manifested in this world in the Fibonacci sequence in nature and human life. It is also called 'The Divine Proportion' or 'The Golden Ratio'.

These are The Divine's attributes or qualities and signs in this visible world. That can show the Divine's perfection on earth.

You will see incredible things only if you search and learn about the power of your mind.

When you know that you have power, then, that power will control your world and reality.

Then, you will not be a slave anymore; you will be the Master of your present and future.

Cinderella's story is similar to the Blessing's one. She also understood that she had to search for this perfect world.

Blessing wrote this poem:

For all the world

I see you flying in the air with your beautiful smile. Awake, it's time to play.

I see you shining as you clothe the sky in yellow rays with your arms of gold.

All your face glows and I see you through the sun.

You awake the stars and you start a new day, a new beginning.

Suddenly, you arise so the eye can see the red fire that warms the earth with a sound wave word of peace.

Because of your beauty, the winds blow and the birds are singing in harmony.

Peace and love will be eternal,

when you are in tune with the right vibration and with your mind in Paradise.

Chapter 18

Open the eye

Blessing said this to me in my dreams:

'This is the time that you will open the third eye completely. I will tell you how I did and how I knew about Paradise.

In the beginning, I felt trapped, I was going in circles. Around me, everyone was aggressive and taking advantage of me. I had to do something.

The only thing I knew is that I am the only one that can help myself. Nobody can know me more than myself.

One day I had a vision, I saw Paradise. It was important what I saw, and what I knew was incredibly amazing.

I was at peace. I felt attracted to that place. It seemed I saw it before. I also knew I was going to be there and that many others were coming.

I was running toward it like Cinderella ran.

It was a place of great joy. I can't describe it with words. It is an intense feeling of peace, there is no sound.

Nothing else was more important than being in that place. I knew I was safe, with great peace and intense joy.

Sometimes things are difficult to understand but you need to learn about them. I knew it was real and perfect.

However, it is so sad that many can only trust what they can see.

They put their trust in what they were told is 'normal' and what they were told is the truth.

Some others, only believe something if it fits with what their other friends and family think and believe. They don't try to think by themselves, they are indoctrinated.

Their minds are polluted by beliefs without a clear explanation or logic. They repeat what was taught without questioning it.

If they decide to change their beliefs, then that will be terrible because they will not fit in with the other friends' beliefs anymore.

However, I had to be strong and question everything to arrive to know what was my truth.

After these experiences, I knew I have to do my journey alone.

Sometimes I was a little sad and I couldn't understand why I was alone in this situation.

It was something I had to learn by myself.

I will know what to do at the right time.

One day, an unexpected angel came to help me. He was showing me things of the spiritual world. I had to learn day by day.

I was not alone any more. I knew that it was for a reason. I had to learn about my inner power and I didn't trust anybody but my angel.

I could never forget the Paradise experience. It was very powerful and beautiful.

Many will come, billions of us will be in Paradise and they will want to fly with us.

The way to Paradise is to have wisdom, and knowledge, and to change your mindset. Open the spiritual eye, not the physical eyes.

In your mind, you have the third eye, the pineal gland which is the antenna to communicate with the Divine.

He is the power and wisdom to know everything and to manifest it.

Reality is what you can't see, the impossible will be possible for you.'

Chapter 19

Magical water

I know that today will be a great day. My friends and my mum are gathered together near the river. We are like stars, and we are all together shining.

Suddenly we heard Blessing and she said, 'Go to the spiritual waters'

When we opened the third eye, we saw the waters in front of us.

Blessing said to all of us, 'Whoever drinks this water will have eternal life. Your beliefs will disappear and the truth and wisdom will be within you.'

And as we drank it. We experienced peace and joy and we felt we were in Paradise.

I was in ecstasy, in a place full of peace and immense love, it was overwhelming.

I saw an aura that was all around us pulsing and shining over our heads.

It was quiet, and there were no negative thoughts in our minds. I was relaxed, comfortable, and safe.

I heard music at 432 Hz, I knew it is a miracle and healing vibration.

Blessing was speaking to our minds.

We sat in a circle holding hands in peace, and we were all on the same synchronicity and vibration.

We heard Blessing said, 'I bless the earth with peace and love so that everyone will receive the same knowledge and wisdom to see who you really are.

You are Light, Energy, and Power. These are the Divine's attributes within you.

You are a Spirit, and you have the Divine's qualities.

You can do anything when you know your power.

The way to achieve this is by knowing who you are and it will be manifested on earth. You have power in your mind to control your destiny.'

Everyone listened with attention. The excitement was great. I can see another reality.

Suddenly, everybody was in silence. We can perceive that something was going to happen.

Blessing said, 'There is only one way to fly. Please, hold hands, in silence and close your eyes, you only need the 'third eye' to guide you.

See yourself flying. Think that it is going to happen. Don't doubt, believe and know this.'

I knew we are all strongly aligned with our souls. We are on the right path.

Blessings said, 'When you want something and you search for it and you find it, then it will come to pass.

Open the third eye, the one with the power that can show you the spiritual world.

Then, tell yourself you can fly, that you have the power to do it, that you can do anything, and that nothing is impossible for you.

See yourself as who you really are, a Soul. Be bold and strong, do not fear anything.

The reflection you always see in the water by the river when you go to drink water is not who you really are. You are more powerful than that.

You are not only that body; you are a spiritual force, a soul that can't die, and that will live forever.

If any of you doubt, please step aside. You need to be strong-minded and confident.'

At that moment, I saw with the third eye that everybody was glowing with an intense light. We were shining, and I have never seen a light so bright in my life.

It was so bright and powerful that I couldn't even move. I was paralysed, but I could hear everything that was happening around me.

Suddenly, I heard that something happened; one by one were having a sort of transformation.

I heard a rustling sound like when you unwrapped a present, but it was not exactly that. My eyes were closed, and I couldn't open them to see what was happening.

Then, I knew what it was, we were all growing *wing*s and we were opening them. But they were not real wings; they were the spiritual wings to fly.

I was so happy that I was going to fly. The atmosphere was peaceful, I could feel some music and the words of glory. I could hear angelic voices in the distance.

All of us were in silence; I could only hear the display of the wings and a very faint song.

At this moment, I screamed repeatedly:

Freedom! Freedom!

Now I understand the Allegory of 'The Cave' by Plato.

I realise that I was in a cave full of man made knowledge and beliefs. It was not the Ultimate Truth.

Now I completely understand that I was not free before, it was all an illusion.

Then I knew I was free of all wrong beliefs and teachings. They told me that I can't fly, that what is real is only what I see, but it is the opposite.

However, at that moment, I was in Paradise. I felt the immense peace that there is in this place.

I understood that the reflection you always see in the water by the river when you go to drink water is not who you really are.

I am more powerful than that.

I have perceived Light. I felt my body lighter, my wings moving, and my body was in a different state.

However, I can't explain exactly what that feeling was. I was experiencing sensations and emotions that I couldn't comprehend but they were real.

Without opening my eyes, I could notice where I was. I didn't need to talk I could communicate with my mum and friends only using telepathy.

I was so happy that all of them were experiencing the same. I have always wanted to fly and be in Paradise. My dream came true.

I can see a New Beginning for the Earth.

This was more beautiful than I thought.

I saw my mum and all my friends so happy, which gave me immense joy. Not only I am in Paradise but also whom I love.

Paradise is real and it will be forever and ever.
We are all experiencing eternal love and peace.

Wisdom manifested Paradise on earth.

Whatever you want you can have it and will be real. You can create peace in this world and whoever will know this wisdom will be with us in Paradise.

Nothing is better than this. Nothing at all.

It doesn't matter how long I have waited for this; I enjoyed every day waiting for Paradise.

This can be your destiny as well.

This is going to be forever, and this is the perfect place that I have dreamt about. It is not a dream anymore, because now I know that it is real.

I am flying! I am in Paradise!

I can see my friends there and they were dancing and rejoicing.
There is music and everyone is happy.

We are clapping, going towards a bright portal made of obsidian and we are all together.

We all shout, 'We have arrived in Paradise and it will be forever and ever.'

I see billions of other people coming and I know that I will help them to know this wisdom so that they can be here.

When YOU have wisdom you will also be in Paradise.

Paradise is not a place it is a change mindset and is where your transformation will begin but only if YOU want to **know** it.

We should be like ants. We should work towards the same goal all together doing and knowing the same so that we can be in Paradise on Earth.

Then, when billions will **know** and have wisdom, they will also be in Paradise on Earth and they will have a New Beginning.

The time is near; you need to be in the same mindset. You should know who you are so that you can be also here.

Put all your concentration on wisdom. Switch everything off that can distract you from knowing this.

Contemplate your thoughts and renew them, they are YOUR thoughts and you can do with them whatever you want, then you should manifest Paradise.

Find peace in your mind and life.

Remember who you are. Remember!

Now you know the truth. The truth is, that it is possible to be in Paradise if you have a connection with the Divine's wisdom.

I want you to be in this eternal life.

I want you to be with me in Paradise.

This is why you are here right now.

Because there are no coincidences in life, nothing is happening by chance not even that you are in this dimension now.

Be in Paradise now!

Renew and examine your beliefs and you will find that the truth is hidden and it is not in plain sight. Remember!

Wisdom will answer all your questions because that is the only way to know the unknown.

'THE UNKNOWN CAN BE KNOWN' (PLATO).

Come with us!

We are waiting for you!

Who told you that you are that which dies?

Legends never die, they live forever...

About the Autor

Gabriela was born in Argentina with an Italian heritage.

She is a multi-lingual Translator, a Theologian, a Language teacher and a writer.

She loves swimming, horse riding, tennis, jokey, and other sports.

She is learning Neoplatonism and she loves it.

In her writings she expresses her knowledge of Plato's teachings and others who inspired her.

She lived in Argentina most of her life.

Subsequently, she lived in Italy for ten years, and now she lives in England.

One day she was inspired to start writing a book to help others on their new journey for a new life and a New Beginning.

Her second book of the Trilogy is about the miracles she saw and she experienced in her life.

There are words of wisdom for you to realise who you are.

About the Book

The book is a self-help and self-improvement short story.

It includes different stories, containing knowledge, wisdom, and true spiritual meaning of reality.

Lucas and his friends are looking for a New Beginning in their lives.

Lucas finds the Truth to help the world.

Are you ready to join him?

Printed in Great Britain
by Amazon

34439649R00076